CISTERCIAN STUDIES SERIES: NUMBER FIFTY-EIGHT

SERMONS IN A MONASTERY ❧

CHAPTER TALKS BY MATTHEW KELTY

CISTERCIAN STUDIES SERIES: NUMBER FIFTY-EIGHT

SERMONS IN A MONASTERY ?❧

CHAPTER TALKS BY MATTHEW KELTY

Edited, with an introduction by
WILLIAM O. PAULSELL

Cistercian Publications, Inc.
Kalamazoo, Michigan
1983

Sermons in a Monastery is Number Fifty-eight
in the Cistercian Studies Series.

Cistercian Publications
WMU Station
Kalamazoo, Michigan 49008

Available in Britain and Europe from
A.R. Mowbray & Co Ltd
St Thomas House   Becket Street
Oxford   OX1   1SJ

Typeset by the Carmelites of Indianapolis

CONTENTS ह•

INTRODUCTION ❧

MATTHEW KELTY is gradually becoming recognized as an important spiritual teacher and counselor. This has been known for a long time by his many friends around the world. It has been discovered by those who have visited and made retreats with him. Now through the printed word more people are able to draw upon his experience.

He has published very little, which is natural for one who feels called to obscurity and solitude. He has had an occasional article in monastic journals and written an excellent piece on Thomas Merton which appeared in *Thomas Merton: Monk*, edited by Patrick Hart.[1] *Letters from a Hermit* is a brief biography of Matthew with a collection of his letters written to the author.[2] *Flute Solo*, written by Matthew,[3] contains reminiscences of his life. It was composed in just a few days while he sat on the beach near his hermitage in Papua New Guinea. This collection of homilies is being presented that more people may learn from his interior wisdom.

A brief biography is in order for those who do not know Matthew Kelty. He was born in 1915 in a Boston suburb that was largely a Protestant area in a heavily Catholic city. The Roman Church had its impact, however, and in 1934 Matthew joined a missionary order, the Divine Word Society. He took his first vows in 1941 and was ordained in 1946. His first assignment was to a primitive land, New Guinea. Arriving in 1948 to assist an older missionary, he made trips into the bush to give instruction, offer mass, and dispense medicine. The life was hard.

[1] New York: Sheed and Ward, 1974; revised and augmented, Kalamazoo: Cistercian Publications, 1983.
[2] Springfield, Illinois: Templegate Publishers, 1978.
[3] Kansas City: Andrews and McMeel, 1979.

There were no modern conveniences, and the loneliness was a heavy burden.

In 1951 Matthew returned to the United States to edit his order's magazine, *The Christian Family*. As readers of this book will discover, Matthew has exceptional gifts in the use of the written word. Still, he was dissatisfied with his life and began to feel a call to the cloistered monastery. Providentially, a fire in the magazine office led to suspension of publication. He made a retreat at the Abbey of Gethsemani in Kentucky, a Cistercian or 'Trappist' house, and decided to enter.

Matthew's two years of novice training were under the direction of Thomas Merton, one of the most productive and popular spiritual writers of the twentieth century. Merton did much to popularize the monastic life, and was Gethsemani's best known monk. In his last years his confessor was Matthew Kelty.

Matthew's days were occupied with the usual monastic activities. He went to choir seven times a day to chant the Divine Office. He worked as the monastery cobbler. Eventually he became Director of Vocations and wrote a little booklet for prospective monks called 'Aspects of the Monastic Calling'. Later, he was spiritual director of the lay brothers and sub-prior. He found his place in the community very quickly, and his talents and experiences were appreciated.

Yet Matthew was still not completely fulfilled. While he will tell anyone that he found everything he went to the monastery for and loved the place deeply, he began to feel drawn to a deeper solitude. The possibilities of the hermit life began to intrigue him. He started spending time in an old pump house at Gethsemani that he converted to a hermitage. He wanted to get down to the basics of life and felt that living in a primitive place might be the solution to his problem. His thoughts went back to his New Guinea experience. The solitude that had once depressed him now appeared more attractive. An invitation from the Bishop of New Guinea to return and live in a hermitage was irresistible.

Negotiating this change with his monastic superiors, however, was difficult. His abbot knew that Matthew was an outgoing, free spirit who might find solitude destructive to his vocation and his personality. There were many long conversations, but no direct approval of the move. Finally, in 1970, a compromise was reached.

Gethsemani had recently taken over a small monastery near Oxford, North Carolina. It had been founded by a French Benedictine and was set up to handle no more than half a dozen monks. The abbot of Gethsemani wanted to see if the 'Trappist' life could be lived in a small group setting and asked Matthew if he would take a few monks to Oxford to experiment. It would not be pure solitude, but the possibilities of a small community of three or four monks were not unattractive.

On 24 June 1970, the feast of John the Baptist, Matthew and two brothers from Gethsemani arrived in Oxford. Within a few weeks they worked out a simple routine. They would pray the psalms in the little chapel three times a day, they would support themselves by weaving, and they would generally maintain silence except at the noon meal, when they would discuss the business of the community.

It was a lonely life without the usual supports one finds in a more traditional Cistercian monastery. The men wore no habits, they had no music; the buildings were simple wooden structures, utilitarian and unattractive. The two brothers left after a few months, Other monks came and stayed for a while, but eventually they too left. Finally, Matthew was by himself, but with more buildings to maintain than just his own hermitage.

There were other problems. He had conflicts with the local bishop. The war in Viet Nam was raging, and Matthew walked to Washington, D.C. as a protest. This brought criticism from those who felt a monk's place is in his cell.

Still, the little monastery was attractive to many people. Contemplative communities have a way of becoming known to those who need them, and many visitors came by, often for extended retreats. These included a psychologist from a nearby university, a member of a religious order that had a house on the Bowery in New York, a Brooklyn policeman, a college religion professor, a young man hitchhiking from Wisconsin to Alaska who wanted to spend a few days at Oxford. There were frequent guests from eastern North Carolina, many of them students. Some were troubled, others simply wanted a few days retreat from the normal pressures of living. All found themselves enriched by their stay.

Matthew had a good life in many ways, and he certainly made life better for those who came to know him. But he could not get New Guinea out of his mind. Unexpectedly, a new abbot at Gethsemani re-opened the question, and Matthew was given permission to go. On 19 November 1973, he left New York by ship and arrived in New Guinea on Christmas Eve.

For a while he lived in a mission station, but eventually he had a hermitage built. He had some visitors and did a small amount of apostolic work on special occasions. Periodically he would visit a monastery in the Philippines or return to Gethsemani to stay in touch with the rest of the world and his Order, but he saw his primary vocation as that of a hermit. Now, having lived that life for almost ten years, he has returned to Gethsemani to take up community life once again. He brings with him the experience of solitude and all that he has learned from it. That, no doubt, will enrich the monastery. The future, for Matthew, always includes the unexpected.

The sermons in this collection were all preached while Matthew was a monk at Gethsemani. They were written specifically for monks, not for a secular audience. A few of them were given when he led retreats in other monasteries. Some were mimeographed, some were crudely typed, some were written in longhand on scrap paper. It is impossible to date most of them, although a few have obvious connections with events, such as the dedication of a remodeled abbey church. Others are related to the Christian year.

Matthew's style of writing is free-flowing, almost stream of consciousness. Incomplete sentences are frequent, and have their rhetorical impact. These sermons were intended more for preaching than for reading. A few have been taped, but are not readily available.

He has a way of taking simple, commonplace things and using them to explain religious truth. The actions of a stray dog reflect the loving presence of the Mother of God. The experiences of a European abbot known for his love of liturgy at a time when the abbey church was being remodeled and could not be used reveal the ironies of the human condition. The death of brother electrician raises questions about the providence of God.

Certain themes dominate this collection. A major one is the human need to balance masculine and feminine elements in a healthy personality. The growing interest in solitude is evident. The nature of the monastic life is discussed in several pieces where the aisle between the choir stalls is called Desolation Row from a Bob Dylan song, and the psalms are described as pictures of human nature.

We are told of various personalities in the monastery, of the deaths or anniversaries of some of the monks. There is a letter that Matthew sent to friends about the death of Thomas Merton. A seasonal homily on 'The Three Wise Men' is actually about Abraham Lincoln, Daniel Boone, and the American cowboy.

Matthew said a few things in these sermons that he no longer holds. He criticized the desire for small communities and simple liturgies, yet these are what he had at Oxford. He told of a monastic life that has since softened its rules and no longer uses Latin. The basic outlook, however, remains the same: seek God and love him.

The sermons tell of life in an American monastery in the 1960s and of one man's growing attraction to solitude. The reader will find Matthew entertaining but provocative. Above all, he calls us to search for God and find him in the simple things of everyday living.

When Matthew left for Papua New Guinea he sent me a large cardboard box of his personal papers. Included were letters, pages of journals, and these sermons. Editing them has rekindled a friendship that flourished during his Oxford years when I taught at a college in North Carolina.

I am grateful to Matthew for his friendship and spiritual guidance. I am also grateful to my wife, Sally, who knew Matthew well, encouraged this project, and proofread the final manuscript.

William O. Paulsell
Lexington Theological Seminary
Summer, 1981

✒ The Monastic Life

THE POOR MONK ೭ು

M ANY MONKS, myself included, are not without their misgivings in the matter of retreat—going on retreat, having a retreat master, making a retreat. There is something to it. Still, my own experience has been that, all my fussing notwithstanding, I have derived a certain benefit from the annual exercise. Perhaps it is no more than a carryover from younger days when the retreat used to be the normal way to begin a scholastic year, approach the taking of vows and the receiving of holy orders, and thus bound to have overtones that color my current approach. Perhaps that is the point: this business of overtones and living in many dimensions at once.

To me, the monastic life has but one purpose and that is to discover √ reality. In order to do that, one must remove from one's vision what is false and fraudulent, the artificial and the constructed. Almost everyone wants to do this, so monks are not freaks for wishing to discover the truth. However, it is far more difficult than it would seem, and that is why not everyone is willing to go to the trouble of being a monk or, even once in the area, willing to stay with it. It is hard. Let us face it, it is hard.

Why should it be so hard to discover the truth? What is there about life that tends to make it something lacquered over and covered up, something filled with pretending and hiding? Why are we so determined to be unreal? Why are we not willing and able to be what we are?

I am not sure I know the answer, but I think it is because we are scared to death that things are the way they seem. And what does that mean, scared to death? Well, we're scared of living and scared of dying. We fear death and sickness, lightning and storm, disaster and wild winds blowing. We fear one another and are afraid of God. We do not trust

3

anyone, not the superior, not our brother, not ourselves. We never know what they are going to do to us. Nor can I trust myself, full of confusion and mixed-up emotions and deceptive ways and skillful manoeuvers. Why, even when I am sure that I am pure as water and as apparent as glass, I have to stop and wonder whether it is not just an act I am putting on.

It's the way it was with Brother. He was young and went about his business like any other monk. Only they made him an electrician because the monk who had been the electrician before him got the idea that there was nothing to do but listen to God telling him to get out of the monastery. He did, and God be with him, but that left us without an electrician.

I do not know how you do it, but our method is direct. When you run out of something, you call a relatively simple, unassuming and submissive monk and you tell him, 'Brother, you are now the electrician'. A few facts, such as he knew nothing about electricity, proved only that the Brother was being irrelevant, and if there is anything one must be these days it is relevant. So Brother said OK, he was the electrician.

He did all right and bravely went about the monastery changing light bulbs and bit by bit advancing into more mysterious areas. The only blunder I know of was when he pulled a plug out of the side of something in the cheese plant and released the ammonia in the refrigerating unit, which could have been bad but did no more than strip three big trees in back of the library and kill them outright. So Brother kept doing his job like anyone else.

One day an X-ray truck came and offered to take our pictures, so we all had our lungs photographed. A few months later the results came back. Brother had on his lungs funny spots over which many doctors frowned many times. So they took him to Louisville, and the grim word came back. They opened him up and took one look and sewed him together again. He was full of cancer. Figure that out and you won't be scared any more.

And there was a friend I knew down in Maine where we used to go summers when I was a kid. The depression was a long while hitting my family, and when it hit, it hit good. But we were doing all right then and saw that the depression arrived in Maine early. My friend worked with his dad in the quarries and so could not go to high school. He made four cents for each cobble stone he made from granite. I never knew such a poor family. They were poor poor. Swedes. The mother was Irish but her faith had not survived. But he grew up a good man and made his way in the world and ended up in Massachusetts a very happy and successful real estate man. He married and had a lovely girl and handsome boy. The boy grew up and went to war, as boys do, to Viet Nam. They hoped he would come back and they wrote me to pray that he might. Well, he didn't. They took it pretty hard, having only middle American faith in God. But they made do. And one day the dad was coming home from work and pulled off the side of the road to get something out of the trunk and some kid came along and ran into him. He was six months on his back in the hospital and came home with one leg gone. You have to work real hard to figure that out. It is one reason we are scared.

It is a hard day for many people. It is a world full of mystery and darkness. The Lord made the night too long for some people. And that is only the beginning.

It is possible to come to terms with the world around us. You can work it out that you get enough to eat, that you are housed and clothed and provided for. You can see that your hospital bills are paid and your children get an education. With a little luck and a lot of struggle you can manage it. Many do. Not all. But many make it.

Yet something gets lost somehow in the process. Many of my generation literally sold their souls in order to get from this world what they thought was coming to them, only to find their children did not want it. It is no small blow to work all your life to give something to your own and then have them tell you to your face that they don't want it, that it means nothing to them, absolutely nothing. And your son and your daughter dress like tramps and live like them and bum their way around the country they loathe, content only to ask for a little money now and then.

So even if you make it, you don't get anywhere; that is clear. And then rising out of your own depths is a voice too strong to strangle: the kids may be right, they have a point. All this world's goods have not brought me genuine happiness. The kids are screwy but they are wiser than I am.

The monk got this message early. His style was a bit neater, and he did not have to go through all the antics of hair and beads. But he got the word and got it soon that what the world offers is not much. There must be something better.

He located a monastery where men live who think roughly the way he does, that if we gang up and go it together we can manage on little enough of this world's goods and still get from it what we need. If we go it alone we may be able to be strong enough to lick the love game and walk through the sex heaven and keep going into the land of freedom. There ought to be a way to meet the will of God head-on and direct, not by standing around waiting for it to happen to you, but by anticipating it, by walking right into it. There ought to be a way to get the jump on God and put yourself so wholly at his disposal that even he cannot help smiling. You are wise to him.

Very well. You came so far. The world did not catch you. The flesh did not take you. You are one with the will of God. This is indeed to master life and to come to know its secret. It is indeed.

Then what? Well, having gone out into this marvelous desert of freedom, you look around you. There are two beings: one is you and the other is God. All is loveliness for a long time as you bask in the sunlight of his glorious presence. It is only gradually that something new is added to this already satisfactory situation. The added note is insight.

The newly-invited guest is so taken up with the beauty of the place and the graciousness of his host that he is not aware of his own gross appearance, his lack of breeding, his awkward manners, his wretched impression. And as it gradually dawns on him, the first impulse is flight. But the host will not let him go, begs him to remain, assures him of his love, promises that all will be well with him. And he waits and watches to see if you believe him, if you are willing to hold your ground and abide with your misery.

And then begins earth's loveliest dialogue, the most beautiful of all love stories. There begins an affair that has no end, the sweet exchange of intimacies between pauper and prince. Nothing ever written has been able to capture it, reproduce it, or convey it. Of this every human love affair is but a faint echo, a small version, a sample and test run.

The capacity of the human heart for this sort of love is infinite, for the human soul is immortal. All human passion for gain, for conquest, all intoxication and high estate, all surrender and submission, are gestures in the right direction, but are not enough. They are futile efforts.

And yet in order to enter the heart one must pass through the very fires of hell, the dragon's pit, and deep dark waters. Of this, people are indeed frightened. The greatest single obstacle on the way to God is fear. We are literally frightened to death. We fear God, people, ourselves, time, eternity, life, and death. Monks too know fear. But in the spirit of God they must go ahead anyway. Otherwise, they do not walk the road of the first Beatitude: Blessed are the poor in spirit. For this is what it is to be poor in spirit.

To be poor means to know what one really is before God, to stand ✓ alone, naked, wretchedly poor before the Lord.

And far more than that. You have gone into the depths of your own heart and have come to know what is there; the region of darkness, the deep where the monsters dwell, the hell into which Christ descended after death on the cross before he rose on the third day. You must not only die with him. You must descend into the depths with him if you are to rise. This is what the monk does.

It is not hard to do. I mean you have only to live here and let the place happen to you. The night, the loneliness, the silence, the remoteness, the seclusion, the emptiness, the poverty, the futility, indeed the silliness of your life. Let that happen to you and you will learn soon enough what man is. And who you are.

Being poor in dollars and cents is good indeed, and we must experience that. But we cannot stop there. We take that with us as we journey into a region of far greater want. The poor in spirit dwell further in, on down the road, where only mad people dwell and wild owls screech in the night.

That is what I mean by living in two dimensions: the business of overtones. For nothing is only what it seems to be. We never live on one level only. If it is a bell at all, it will ring with hundreds of tones when you strike it. You just have to be willing to hear them. No life is dimensionless, no life without overtones. Infinite ones. Divine ones. And they are part of reality, the best part, the main part, the part that matters.

For it is not that life is wretched that makes it real. It is not that we are poor that makes us matter. Monks are not more because they are simple, plain folk living back in the hills. No, it is seeing what is there that makes us human. It is the ability to grasp total reality that makes the monk. Everything else is just equipment and tools to work with.

Though we are ragged in the extreme, we are the objects of divine love. We are loved, we are loved. And it is our poverty and wretchedness that makes the love so wonderful.

Our ministry to the world is not to be anything other than what we are. In that we discover what is hidden from view: the divine. The presence of God is all around us, in us, among us, in the hills and in the woods, in the blight and the burden, in the sorrow and the laughter. We can laugh then, with Christ, and shed tears with him. Walk on the water, go up to Tabor, enter the garden of olives. With him all the way, all the time. Poor. And ours is the kingdom.

THE PSALMS AS PRAYER ॐ

O UR SUBJECT TODAY is the psalms as prayer. It would seem to me at the outset that the psalms are a very proper form of prayer and a very dangerous one.

Very proper to be sure. People have prayed the psalms from the time they were written. Since first chanted by their authors to our own day, the psalms have been the prayer form of humanity. Christendom has never been without psalmody. There was no time within the last three thousand years when psalmody was not heard on earth. There is no part of the globe today where the psalms are not on someone's lips.

The Jews in official and unofficial worship, John the Baptist, the apostles, Mary the Mother of God, the Lord himself, monks of Palestine, of Egypt, of Ireland, of Gaul, bishops and monsignors and missionaries, Protestants, the Orthodox, popes, all prayed the psalms. There is no gainsaying the fact that the psalms are proper prayer.

And yet the average Catholic today, I venture to suggest, does not pray the psalter. Does your father? Your mother? You do, as a priest, as a monk, as one officially involved in the prayer of the Church. Do you suppose that of those who have been here for a time and later decided to leave, do you suppose many of them continue to pray the psalms? Are the psalms so much a part of you now that no matter what strange circumstances might overtake you in the Providence of God, the psalms would never leave you? In both instances I believe the reply would be positive in large numbers. And yet hardly representative of the Catholic world as a whole.

Thus, though the psalms in Holy Church have had in all her history a queenly place in formal prayer, it must be admitted that the psalms have not always entered deeply into the prayer life of the faithful.

The reason is not hard to see. Most people do not consciously live on the level of the psalms. Consequently they do not find the psalms true. They find them archaic, extremist, dramatic, overwrought, frantic. Many people do not pray the psalms because they simply do not feel the way the psalms feel.

Maybe it is just as well. When people do not choose to go deep within themselves they may have their reasons. The wilderness was too much for the early Kentuckians and they never mastered it. They were mastered by it. Even before the lumber boom and the coal companies. Contact with elemental forces has a way of reducing life to fundamental questions. The sea, the mountains, the desert, the wilderness, have all been from ancient times the testing place of the spirit. Some have observed that despair was an abiding element of the Appalachian spirit.

When I maintain that the psalms are dangerous prayer, I mean they are in the same category as silence, solitude, and seclusion. All of these can be dangerous company. So can the Kentucky wilderness, as the book we have been reading in the refectory [Harry Caudill, *Night Comes to the Cumberlands*] tells us. The problems in Appalachia, however, were not caused by the wilderness or its wild beauty or the simple, rugged life of hard work, plain fare, and involvement with elemental things such as wood, water, fire, earth, sky, animals, life, or death. No, it was not these things that brought the people so much unhappiness. It was the evil within themselves which they could not cope with, an evil that burst forth in violence, hatred, despair, that made their lives miserable. Fallen Adam turned loose in Paradise is wretchedly unhappy. Kentucky is still a very beautiful land and in those days it was even more beautiful. The root problem was within the people.

So too contact with the psalter can be dangerous. To me it is a dangerous form of prayer, for when you take the psalms seriously and receive their spirit as your own, when you live what they live and experience what they experience, you come very soon into contact with some basic realities about human nature. The psalms are not all nature hymns and marching tunes, song and dance, the strumming of cithara and the clapping of hands. There is also darkness, wrath and anger, hatred and vengeance, and a host of other unhappy qualities in the heart of a person. Why dangerous? Because if you run into these aspects and recognize them not as something you are reading about but something in your own heart, then what are you going to do about it?

How are you going to cope with the forces you recognize in your own depths? Forces of darkness? What are you going to do when it dawns on you that the words of David are true not only of David, but of you? And having met these monsters, what if you cannot master them? The psalms are indeed strong meat, heavy fare.

Just as the wilderness is. Not everyone who comes to the monastery remains. In the desert you meet demons and you must wrestle with them. The demons are not in the desert, they are in you. But when you venture into the wilderness you discover them.

Where does the answer lie? The answer lies in Jesus. To my mind, unless we pray the psalter with Jesus we had better not pray it at all. Unless we can do so with him who shares our humanity, it were best to leave well enough alone. In entering into the ways of the wilderness, into the mysteries we experience only by contact with solitude and seclusion, we must be grounded deeply in faith, faith in Christ's love for us. It is only in this faith that we can look upon reality and not succumb to despair.

This is the constant concern of monks, for exposed pitilessly to the misery of human nature as we experience it in each other, the temptation to despair is always at hand. It can only be overcome by casting our anxieties on the rock which is Christ, for he has taken all our misery upon himself.

I need hardly add that the Cistercian has with this faith in Christ a tender love for the Mother of God. This he must have. This love for Our Lady keeps one close to the presence of purity, tenderness, and compassion. Without her loveliness we grow harsh.

One might at this point ask, 'Why bother?' If the desert is dangerous, why go out there? Why go into the wilderness? If those people were not strong enough to endure the wilderness of Kentucky, why didn't they stay on the safe side of the mountains? If the psalms are dangerous, why not say mild and gentle prayers?

I don't know why, really. If you want to stay at home, that is all right, I should think. No one has to go to a monastery. But some people somehow, want to know and experience what it is to be human, all the way in, all the way down. And in a sense God calls us to that. For it is only by an experience of ourselves as we truly are that we begin to know the beauty that surrounds us like a light of glory which is the love of God. It is only when we go into the wilderness with Jesus that life begins. Only when we pray the psalms with him that prayer begins, and with it an awareness that without him we are lost.

Thus the monastery exists for one purpose: the contemplative experience. The work, the prayer, the reading, austerity, fasting, charity, poverty—all these are but means to accomplish the one goal: the experience of God. While such an experience can never be produced, let alone legislated, there are conditions which make it possible in the grace of God. The monastery's purpose is to provide these conditions. If it does not, it fails its purpose. If the monastery provides them but the monks do not make use of them, they fail.

Psalmody is one of the traditional roads to that experience of God. Almost any single aspect of the monastic life can be an entry into the mystery of God. Prayer, silence, community service, obedience, sickness, failure, work, solitude—any of these singly or all of them together can be the way to a profound grasp of God. If your heart is pure you will see him, that is sure. You can be just as sure that it will be where you least expect. No one is as unpredictable as God, nor as surprising.

In entering the world of the psalms we touch human nature on all levels. Sometimes it is a joyous, benign contact. Sometimes it is rather dreadful. But there can be no prayer of any depth until we have descended into our own depths. And in the psalms we can do this.

If I say that the psalter is not too popular, perhaps here is the reason. People do not know, and they do not want to know themselves. They much prefer to live on a fragile surface with a workable bundle of adjustments they pass off to themselves and others as to who they are. Hand such people a psalter and they will be ill at ease with anything except pretty ones about the glory of God and the beauty of nature. But turn to some of the wilder psalms and they find the words inappropriate and the sentiments unchristian. As undoubtedly they are. But until you have penetrated with Christ into your own depths, much of you also is unchristian and will remain so.

The psalms can teach us much of this, of the conflict with evil within us. Bring us face to face with the traitor in our own heart: the two-timer, the time-server, the false friend. Who has not met the demon of envy, of jealousy, of greed, of hatred, lurking in the dark shadows of his depths, a side of himself that rarely comes into the light? And what appropriate ✓ words we find in the psalms to deal with these elements of hell within us! Christ descended into hell and we must descend there with him, into the infernal regions of our own heart.

A monk is called to reality and to the brave look at reality which is given the dignified name of contemplation. There is nothing dignified about fallen humanity, and to contemplate it can lead nowhere except to despair unless we do it in Christ. Thus to enter into psalmody as to enter into the wilderness must be done with Christ.

So we say the psalms with Jesus, all of them, in the long quiet years of manual work, in the solitary days in the desert, on Tabor and in Galilee, walking on the sea and preaching on the hillside, with him on his way to the Holy City, in his struggles with the world, with law and authority, with the establishment, with him in his betrayal, his suffering and death, in his descent into hell, and in his glorious rising, until he comes again at the end. Praying with him in the wilderness of this world unafraid, rooted in faith and in his love.

THERE MUST BE AN ELEMENT
OF MADNESS IN OUR LIFE ❦

THERE MUST BE an element of madness in our life. However, in saying this, one must make some distinctions. First of all, what madness is not. It is not to think of our monastic life as a kind of joke. It does not mean doing things any old way, in any kind of fashion. It does not mean throwing things around and wasting material and being careless and carefree under the pretext that this is all madness anyway and nothing really matters very much. It does not mean playing high, wide and handsome with rules and regulations. On the contrary it means a great, sober seriousness: a serious approach to prayer, to choir, to work, to reading, to silence, and to everything else that is part of life. If I do not take the life seriously then the joke is on me because the Lord will not take me seriously when I come at the end, knocking on his door. 'I know you not', he will say, 'nor do you know me'. It does not mean this madness—a want of obedience, a desire to live the life on my own terms, in accord with my own desires, mad to be sure, but with my own version of madness.

It is true, I know, that many spiritual writers, as well as others, have referred to human existence as something of a joke, but we cannot tell how or in what way until it is all over. Life may be truly something of a joke, but on this side of the eternal curtain we do not know what the joke is. We do not know for sure where the irony lies, where the incongruity is hidden, nor can we detect it. What we must do is take it all quite seriously, since no game is worth playing unless the players really play. If we do not, we may spoil it all for ourselves and others and the riddle of life will then never be answered. We shall spend eternity in a kind of hell where everyone is laughing and we alone do not get the joke.

What is madness then? I should think it could be called a way of doing things, an outlook on life, a *Weltanschauung* as the Germans so beautifully say, a way of looking at the world. It is the context in which we fulfill our own role in the world. An approach to life, a mood, a setting. Madness is commonly thought to be characteristic of lovers. The lover is said to be 'madly in love'. All true love has an element of madness about it, an element of the unreasonable, the extreme, the romantic. I think it is only this kind of love that really touches the heart of a woman. Every true leader has an element of madness that inspires followers with a passionate loyalty. All the saints had a kind of madness, a passion in their love for God that gave their lives great drive and fire, intensity and power. A great saint, a great leader, a great mind, a great scientist, a great person in any field has a kind of madness with which one devotes oneself wholeheartedly to one's call in life. It is part of greatness.

What is specific about madness, what distinguishes it, say, from simple enthusiasm and ardor, is its refusal to submit everything to cold reason as the ultimate norm. The saints and the great of the earth realize that there comes a time when reason and reasonableness are useless. Then they step over reason, go beyond it, operate above the areas and range of the human mind. They have even to be unreasonable. And in so doing they turn out in the end to be the most reasonable of all. *La raison pour l'amour c'est l'amour.*

What is monastic about madness? Or better, in what way are monks mad? I think the whole monastic life is mad. I think this is a mad house, full of mad men. Shall I mention some of the mad things that go on here? What these monks do? They go off into the wilderness, put up a wall, stay behind it, keep the world out. They get up at 2:00 in the morning. They spend hours every day singing songs to God in an ancient and forgotten tongue and melody. They wear great cowls and cloaks when they sing them. They are celibate, virginal; they never marry, have no wives, no children. They live in one place and never leave it. They do not talk as others talk. They do not eat as others eat. They do not sleep as others sleep, but clothed, on planks and straw, in a common room. They drink no beer, watch no TV, play no games, never sit around and chat. They live subject to authority, whose whim or wish, whose order or command is law, binding not only in the practical order, but also in the realm of soul and spirit. They live in peace with each other, do not fight, do not strike back, bear correction, suffer wrong, endure insult, turn the other cheek. They work hard where told, as told, when told. And lots more.

Do not tell me this is not madness. I do not care how good the cheese is that they make, how splendid the fruit cakes; they are mad. The people who do these things must be out of their minds. Or else they are in love. That is it, of course. They are in love. They do mad things because people who are in love do mad things. There is no other way that love can speak. This is the language of love. It is not necessary. It is not reasonable. It is not in accord with common sense. All very true. It is simply the way of people who are in love. That is all.

You can love another way, to be sure. You can make love reasonable. You can make love have sense. You can tone it down. You can make it prudent and sane. People have been doing this all through history, certainly through the history of religion. There have always been two camps in the people of God: those who wish to love a reasonable service and those who want to make it mad. I was hungry for a little madness. So I came here. And I found it.

Why are some called to a life of this kind? Why do some people find a reasonable service satisfying? And others do not? I do not know. That is a mystery hidden in God. But I can tell you why I had a need for madness.

When I led a reasonable life in which everything made sense it followed by the very nature of things that the God I knew and loved and served was also reasonable. He was good and kind and tender and merciful and, most of all, reasonable. That he was fashioned after my own image and likeness does not matter, for had he appeared to me in any other guise I simply would not have recognized him. I would not have known him. In all his relations with me he was always exactly as I expected him to be. He was the kind of God I wanted him to be.

Where the trouble started was with the people, the common people of the world, the faithful, as we say. I served them, worked for them, and brought to them the God I knew and loved. But he had a way of dealing with them that was not in accord with the way that I drew him. I met misery everywhere and found it impossible to keep the kind of

God I knew alive. I met death and disease and anguish of every kind: men with no work, families whose fathers simply walked out on them, wives who lost their minds, mothers whose little children were taken in death, men and women putting up with dreadful conditions in their families, their homes, their neighborhoods, their work, their parishes, and having to put up with them, simply having to live with them. All these were good people, not wretched sinners living in vice and debauchery, but good, good people. And when God would permit all these things they would cry for a while and then wipe their tears and accept the will of God because they loved him.

When I tried to console them with talk about the God I knew and loved, I could not. My God was kind and reasonable and good and benign. He never did things like that.

I thought I had better change my God. I did. I came here. I thought this place was mad and full of monks loving a God who was also mad. And then I suddenly realized the meaning of it all. When your life in grace is governed by reason and the reasonable beyond a certain point you lose your touch with God. You are out of context with him. You no longer speak his language. When he speaks you do not hear him. When he acts you do not comprehend. You miss entirely the workings of God because you are in the fog of earthly life. But when you operate in the area of madness you begin to speak a language that God speaks. You operate on a level in which God can also operate and in which he can reach you. And so there is contact. Where there is contact with God there is life and there is love. So madness is what puts you in proper context, makes it possible for you to reach God. That is why it is so important. For the monk this is all the more important, since the main things in a monk's life go on in his soul. These things are not settled by human reason. They are not reasonable.

God is not only a God of light, he is also a God of darkness. He is not only the child in the crib, he is also the man gone to a hideous death on the disgraceful cross. He is not only the Christ that John leaned on in love, he is also the Lord God Almighty Who will come at the end to judge the living and the dead. God is simply not sensible and reasonable and fashioned according to our own dimensions. You cannot figure out the ways of God because his ways are not ours. He had his own way of doing things. To the poor human mind these ways seem fantastic and cruel and beyond comprehension. No matter, he is God and we have only to believe in his love for us. The monk in his heart comes to know this God, knows him by experience, and comes to know the meaning of those dark sayings, 'Unless a grain of wheat fall to the ground and die...; he who loves his life will lose it, he who loses it for my sake will find it...; unless a man be born again...; unless you take up your cross and follow me...; unless a man hate father and mother...; if your hand scandalize thee, cut it off... the kingdom of heaven suffers violence and the violent bear it away...'.

But there is in every human heart a constant urge to bring God down to size and make him a God we can fathom, we can reckon with, deal with. People want a God who is reasonable and sensible and understandable. That is why everyone likes Christmas and no one talks of Judgment Day. But God keeps stepping into lives anyway with death and trial and trouble and disease and anguish and misery. And people of faith understand and accept the lesson. Those of no faith despair, I suppose, or hate.

We too try to make God nice. We try to make our life reasonable, try to take the madness out of it. We expect everything to be reasonable. But when the madness is gone, the touch with God is gone, and when God is gone we have only ourselves. Then the life here would be utterly reasonable and as dull as dishwater. And just about as useful.

But it is not just a living out of a life characterized by a number of strange rituals, old customs and monastic traditions, odd usages, that serves to make our life mad. After all, these things can and do change. But they, or something equally mad, must remain if the life is to be of any value and be loyal to its best traditions. As soon as you try to make going out into the desert utterly reasonable, sensible, you have gone there in vain. You might just as well not have bothered. It is not something for the practical minded. It is for the mad.

This monastic setting is not the goal. Rather, it makes it possible for us to embrace the action of God which, to human understanding, is often sheer madness. That means any action of God in our own world: in the rule, the daily order, the wishes and commands of superiors, the flaws and faults and failings of others and of our own doing—the annoyances, frustrations, distresses that are inevitable in a group of people living together. In all this we must find God somehow, or else we are doomed to a dull, meaningless life.

So the question is: what madness characterizes your own life? When was the last time something unreasonable happened to you? When last did something that did not make sense cross your path? When were you last rebuked unjustly? Treated unfairly? Abused by authority? I might just as well ask: when last did God kiss you? Embrace you? For this is the kind of thing that happens every day to the thousands of people we call the faithful. They see the hand of God in all this because they have to. We do not have to. We are invited to. If we do not, we miss the whole point. We do not know God and do not understand how he operates or when he has his arms around us.

The common fisherman in his boat knows more about the ways of God than we, for he knows that God is a God of mystery and deeps and abysses beyond human fathoming, as unknowable as the ways of the sea, the winds, and the weather, the fish in the water. That is why men of the sea are often very wise men. That is why Christ loved fishermen. If we cannot recognize God in the madness of life we have much to learn. And the monastery is a good school.

I came here because I thought this was a mad house full of mad people. It struck me as a house full of those who know love and know what love is about, who are not afraid of God as he is, not as they would like him to be.

The Church has its reasonable people serving a reasonable God in a reasonable way. That seems to be necessary. However, it does seem also that the world meanwhile rolls merrily on. There is need also of the madness of great love, the love of those who know God, know how he works, and can recognize his hand.

We do not have to understand him, but a little madness in our life will help. It will lead us into the depths of the great good Lord, the loving God of mystery, of the Infinite, the child in the crib who will come to judge us all. In this, too, we will keep the common touch that makes us one with our neighbors in kissing the holy hands that lay a cross upon our back.

I do not believe there is a greater joy on earth, for it is to know and be known, to love and to be loved.

But there must be an element of madness in our life.

DESOLATION ROW &

T HERE IS A YOUNG POET and musician named Bob Dylan who, for
the past ten years or so, has had no small impact on our times.
While he inspires both loathing and adoration, I think most admit that his gifts are the great and unusual. One of his best songs is a
piece called *Desolation Row*. Since it is made up of a series of more-or-less
connected, vivid images, the interpretation is bound to vary with different people, even though the total message escapes few. This is part of
the song's power. It gets through to you even when you cannot account
for it.

Listening to it leads me to think that it is the song of love's failure, and
that the admission of failure in love is the beginning of the healing and
the way to genuine love.

The verses describe various characters, some from history, some literary
allusions, some simple types; they cover a wide field. The overall indict-
ment is that they have failed in love. But what happens when these people
begin to discover that they have failed in love? They look for someone to
blame, for someone to punish for their own failures. But Dylan says that
this is not the answer at all. The answer is rather in the admission that you
yourself failed love, and that the desolation you think is the characteristic
of someone else's heart is really your own. You realize that you too live
on *Desolation Row*. To admit this is to shed pretense and to open the way
to a genuine understanding of what love is.

I find it remarkable that so young a man—he was in his early 20s
when he wrote this song—should be so shrewd in his analysis, so keen in
his look into the human heart, so aware of contemporary need. I believe
he would know what I was talking about if I told him that I thought
monastic choir was a lot like *Desolation Row*.

20

In the song they are hanging Cassanova because he failed in love. Often enough we act this out in our lives, seeking a Cassanova we can hang with a good conscience. We hang the abbot, or the house, or the order, or the religious life, or the church, or the priesthood, or the community. Anyone, just so long as it is someone else, for if there is one thing we try by all means to make clear, it is this: *we* do not live on *Desolation Row.*

What do you do when you discover that *Desolation Row* is not only the name of a song, but also the name of the street you live on? What do you do when you discover after years of holy vows that, pledged chastity notwithstanding, you selfishly hunger for affection and seek it greedily and have little genuine love? What do you do when you realize that honestly you have no love at all for poverty, but want as nice a life as you can manage under the circumstances? What do you do when you realize that truthfully speaking you live in a constant fear that someday God may tell you to do something you do not want to do? What do you do when it comes home to you that the field of dry bones is yourself, that the abomination of desolation is you, that Lazarus three days dead in the tomb and stinking is not Lazarus at all, but a person with your name? What do you do when it suddenly dawns on you: I am a resident of *Desolation Row?* What do you do? Why, you thank God and sing out for joy that liberation has come, that the day of redemption is at hand! Discovery that one lives on *Desolation Row* is a common experience today.

However, the response to the discovery is not always one of gratitude to God. Often it is a response of flight. People flee from a marriage, from vows, from sacred orders, from society, with the feeling that in this way they escape from the phoney. They are mistaken. For it is not marriage that is phoney, or the vows of religion, or sacred orders, or society. It is humanity, and humanity is not delivered from the phoney by taking a trip. If anything, this will make even more clear his unreality.

One reason people come to the monastic desert is to discover phoniness, not escape it. When monks begin to discover the dimensions of their own unreality, running does not always seem to be the appropriate answer. Sooner or later you have to stop running.

It seems to me that the acceptance of our desolation is not merely accessory to the monastic life, but is of its very structure. It is that because that is the point of Christ's redemption. Christ's life, death, and rising for us was not an adjustment or tune-up, but our complete and entire rebirth. This rebirth was begun in our death and birth-to-life baptism. It continues all our lives. It is never really complete until our last act by which we at once die and are born to life eternal.

But while we live we are constantly being *put to death* and are *born to life* and the two actions are generally so interwoven and interlaced that it is usually impossible to know what is going on. What we take to be our death may be a new birth, and what we interpret as a new lease on life may be the beginning of the end.

This is certainly true of our residence on *Desolation Row*. Not many are anxious to accept the truth of the situation, and when they do, too often it is thought of as the ultimate catastrophe.

Thus, when monks line up in choir to chant the praise of God, how like a *Desolation Row*, as the two sides of the street face each other and, as it were, leaning out the windows, they eye the scene. What a pity when you think that *Desolation Row* is only the people on the other side! The desolation you look at in others is the desolation they are observing in you from across the street.

What then? We simply stare at another's misery and possibly come to suspect it is also our own?

Indeed not, for that is to miss the whole point. For Christ made *Desolation Row* his road. This is the street he lived on, the way he walked. He made it a Glory Street and paved it with gold. All its creaky residences and all the mixed-up citizenry are aglow with the great light and an everlasting splendor. For *Desolation Row* runs right down the middle of heaven. If it does not, then there is no heaven.

If you do not see the desolation of the street you live on, then it is impossible for you to see its beauty, that is, to see it as it really is. For this is the irony of it. Until you recognize the street as the one you live on, it is just somebody else's *Desolation Row* to you. You live in the suburbs. At least you think you do. But there, of course, the desolation is even worse.

Monks have been standing in choir for fifteen or sixteen centuries, I suppose, and in Gethsemani for a century and more, chanting psalms across the street to one another. There must be something to it for it to last so long. So many other customs have come and gone. There have been eras when multitudes were in choir and times when there was only a handful, times when the action was thought wonderful, times when it was thought useless, a waste. Still, down to this day, monks take their places, take up the psalms and sing across the chasm. There is something here, that is sure.

Oftentimes people come to religious life expecting a place of love, especially love experienced as received. They call this an experience of Christianity. Yet is this valid? Is a Christian community a place found at last where everyone treats you right, where no one insults you, no one presumes upon you, no one takes you for granted? Thus, when a monk throws up his hands in mock horror with the word, 'There is no love in this place', one wonders why he was so long in making the discovery! Christianity is not to find the city of love, but to build it. It is in the building of it that we discover it. 'See how they love one another' was spoken of the Christian community by an outsider. The Christians did not experience it that way. They were busy building love. Generally, we do not begin to love until we learn that we live on *Desolation Row*. After a lifetime of building we think we may have produced at least something, after all the prayer, the sacrifice, the service. But when the light of truth is given us we learn we have built no more than a shantytown.

What do you do then?

Why, you rejoice because victory is at hand. In our defeat lies our triumph; in our ignominy lies our glory. There in the midst of the shambles and ruin that is you the Spirit of God will hover and turn all into a splendid vision.

This is Christianity, to acknowledge that it is Christ who is the Savior. With him we are to live, to suffer, to die, and then go down into the tomb and with him rise.

How long is it going to be before we recognize the street we live on? How long is it going to be before we acknowledge who we are? We are the residents of *Desolation Row*. We are poor, misshapen, misformed, bent, warped, twisted, corrupt.

That is why monastic choir is so glorious and so dreadful. Obviously it is a glory, for to be there is to share in the song of the angels, it is to join the angelic hosts in the praise of God. It is to be robed in white and made rich in love and sing the eternal song of peace and joy. But it is also dreadful, for we see who we are. We look across the avenue at the residents of *Desolation Row* and they look across at us. This is the inner city. This is the dialogue that matters. This is the desert waste, the asphalt jungle and the concrete nightmare. This is Appalachia and Detroit. In this wilderness we take our stand. It is no wonder that people have found this challenge awesome, no wonder they have sought one way or another to abandon so gruelling an enterprise. This is no fairy song and dance routine. What a marvel that it should have perdured!

They tell me that the sound is bad in the church today. That could well be. You suspect it might be so, the sounds being what they are. But the thought has come, perhaps the hearing also is bad? Are people listening? Do they listen for the word, get the message? Maybe they *want* the acoustics to be poor. In the great choir of the world how chaotic must things become before people recognize what they are and where they live? How loud do the speakers have to be before people hear?

Why not listen a little? Why not slow down some, hush up a bit, sit still a moment, turn on your dreams and listen to the wind, to the woods, to the water? Bend over and look down into the dark pool of your own depths and do not be afraid.

As time moves on with us I suspect the message may get louder. The evidence already great will grow greater. How good it will be at that time if you are able to help because in your own heart you have already experienced the awesome anguish of discovering that you live on *Desolation Row*.

We take ourselves as we are and we take others as they are and together we take a stand for love. All the evidence to the contrary notwithstanding, love is all that matters. It is only love that makes *Desolation Row* a Glory Road. Love is already there. That is where he lives.

The hippie movement may have developed because monks were not doing what they were called to do. There is something poignant about it. Though we may shake our gray heads over dope and dirt and debauchery, there was more to it than that. We believe in love, do we not? Is not love the most important thing in the world to us? We too have turned our backs on the affluent society and the social whirl and the cocktail party and Madison Avenue and suburbia. We too believe in prayer and mysticism and contemplation and ecstasy. We too believe in poverty and trust and Providence. We too use bells and incense and beads, and we too have dispensed with worldly clothes and pay no attention to fashions. We too are rebels against the whole of modern society and we too are sick to death of war and bloodshed and violence and hatred. We too are flower children. Perhaps the hippie movement was a stinging rebuke to us that we are not getting through, perhaps a word of encouragement to us. How great must be the need for the kind of thing we are trying to do if the very children cry out for it!

It is when we begin to discover the dimensions of the loveless world around us, the loveless world of our family, the loveless quality of our own heart, that good is born. For this is what can lead us to Christ. Love can come only in Christ. Too often we choose to build the world of love on our own. There is no greater folly. We cannot be our own saviours, no matter how good our intentions. It is rather Christ, dwelling in the midst of our poverty, who is the beginning and the end of love. But so long as we are not willing to encounter our own poverty we will never meet the One who lives in it.

I suggest as many as possible, as soon as possible, plunge into the desolation of their own hearts and learn what it is to be a Christian, to be a sinner in need of redemption rather than a pious person in need of praise. Otherwise the lines of chaos in our world are going to be drawn with an ever-increasing boldness and clarity, so that the very birds of the air and the dogs of the street will know that Desolation is at hand. And even on that day, you may be sure, people will be busy reassuring one another that they can fix it up in short order with a little work and a little luck, and a few adjustments here and there.

There is no joy akin to the joy of knowing the love of Christ, but this joy is impossible unless you know what street he lives on.

Monks have been lining up in choir and waiting for the knock to kneel for the *Ave* here in the Gethsemani church for over a hundred years. It is a great miracle. One can only wonder how long it will continue!

People today are more frightened than ever, so it is no wonder they settle in cozy clusters and gather round the kitchen table in intimate liturgy rather than take a courageous stand in the ranks their fathers so nobly filled. No matter. We can still hope that God will send us people unafraid. After all, the place is named Gethsemani and should attract one who is acquainted with desolation.

THE MONASTIC TECHNIQUE &

EOPLE SOMETIMES take the trouble to go to art school and yet never turn out to be real artists. People take speech courses and never succeed in effective speaking. People study music and spend years in practice, yet when they sit down at the piano nothing really happens. They play everything as it is written and yet it sounds exactly like what it is: a performance. A thing without heart, without life, without spontaneity. It does not come from within. This is not to deny the need for technique, yet techniques do not make the artist. That is clear enough.

It is very necessary that we never forget this. We learn monastic techniques and think this means something. By this process we have somehow managed to get over the wall and into an area that makes us somehow holy. We put on our cowl and sweep by the poor secular; ignorant, unlettered, uncouth, unwise to the ways and mysteries of divine love. Alas!

This is the constant danger for any professional person. A medical training and a medical air do not make a doctor. You can learn all the monastic tricks from the first moment in the morning until the last at night and miss the point of the business. Most of us do not take it that far. We are not that bad. Rather, we pick up some of this and are either not aware of it or else do not succeed in shaking ourselves free of it.

We are great pretenders. We put on airs, a good show. One has the feeling that much seminary training in pre-Vatican II days was heavy in the direction of giving a good example, making a good impression, and not giving scandal. This was no doubt well-intended, but I am sure much of the result was disastrous.

Some of the contempt for religion and the religious life is quite justified. People simply go by what they see. Too often religion is just a veneer over a rather dreadful person.

Our religious life may be no more if we are not very careful. There is a widespread interest today in the contemplative life, but men and women are not turning to the traditional forms of this life today to attain the contemplative experience. This bears watching. Is it only that they do not know about us? Have never heard of us? Quite possibly. But it is also possible that they see nothing of what they are after in what we are doing.

The way to avoid the problem is to live with a real, dynamic, and vibrant sense of the human condition. This sense can come only by contact with our deepest side, the side that most quickly comes into view in the hours of silence and loneliness, in the quiet of the night, in the peace of a natural surrounding. This we must welcome, love, and embrace. It is the key to freedom. Without this contact we run the most fearsome risk of becoming totally unreal, aloof and remote.

We are always up against the temptation to put something on. We do not like nakedness. We do not like to be seen for what we truly are. We grab for anything to give us a little sense of being somebody. Even to be the poorest in the community or the most stupid or the last and the least is something. Or we take our talents, our abilities, our prowess, our aptitudes and use them for all they are worth, for God's glory without doubt, and yet wear the results with a becoming modesty that keeps us very warm in these long winter nights. There is absolutely nothing that we cannot turn to our own account: fast or vigil or prayer or obedience or poverty or service or devotion or stability or perseverance. Anything and everything will do. And yet, to fall for this, to take this seriously, is to betray the whole monastic life. It is to be cheated of the whole point.

The purpose of monastic *ascesis* is to discover reality, not to hide it. If you come out into the desert and there surround yourself with all the clutter of town life you might just as well have stayed where you were. Like the time I was fishing way up in the north woods in some far-away lake and I was thinking how wonderful it was to be so far away in the wilderness. As I was moving along the wooded shore to pick a better spot I stumbled upon two men fishing and they had their transistor radio going full blast with the ball game on from Chicago. How mad can you get? You go all the way to the end of nowhere and take the ball game with you?

In other words, the purpose of the monastery is to set a person free from the domination of things external to him. By going into the monastery one professes a way of life that will lead to liberation from the slavery to passions, to property, to power, to false gods. The results are not guaranteed, but they can be ours. And one of the more subtle dangers is that of being overcome by the technique itself, becoming enslaved to what was to set you free.

It is not just that whereas we once had property of some size, we now fight over a ball point pen, or that we promised the abbot the world and everything in it and are not willing to take on some small chore. It is far more subtle.

It can perhaps be described as the temptation to become the professionally religious person, one who makes a life work of professing religion. This is one's job, one's career. It can be done, and done very well. The lives of such people are sometimes edifying and even inspiring. They give good example. And yet something vital is missing; something very important is left out.

It is something of a game. You have to play the game seriously; if you do not, it is no fun at all. Yet you always have to remember that it is, after all, only a game. It is in the keeping of this neat balance that the secret lies.

In a sense the monastic life is just a game, yet it is something that must be taken very seriously. And yet if you take the game too seriously no one will want to play with you because you are too tight, too closely wrapped up in yourself. You are not free. You are not casual enough. Uptight is perhaps the word. It should be fun, and it is fun when you do it right.

What is the art of doing it this way? It is the art of going more deeply into it and realizing that the point is underneath it all. Behind it. Below it.

There is a kind of woman who keeps so neat a house that no one can live in it. She misses the point. A house is something to live in, not something to keep clean and neat. If she keeps insisting that this is the way she expresses love, you will have to tell her that she doesn't know much about love.

Contact with the inner dimension is essential. If you go on through things to their meaning you reach the main area. It is like people. The individual is not just a hundred sixty-five pounds of flesh and bone, having blue eyes and brown hair and certain features of face and certain characteristics. That is not me at all, that is just the equipment, the framework. I am far more than all these things. I am, in a way, my smile, my look, my walk, my gesture. You can tell a monk even when he is a mile away by the way he looks on the horizon. We know one another that well. I know who is standing next to me even when I do not see who it is. I can tell by the person's presence.

The monastery is not this house, this land, these people, this history. It is that indeed and far more than that. You are not just your daily performance, the clothes you wear, the work you do, the prayers you say, the thoughts you think, the words you utter. You are far more than these. There is a you deep down within, something real and immortal and touched with the divine. Touched, indeed. Possessed by the divine. Loved by the Lord God and wrapped in his presence.

But you are also a person shrouded in darkness in whom strange forces are at war. You are a person tossed by moods and feelings and emotions, tainted with despair and hatred and envy, tempted by pride and ambition and a desire for power. Sometimes these dark forces are frightening. Often not. They may sleep undisturbed in your depths until they are aroused by some event that happens to you. They speak in your dreams. They come out in actions quite unknown to yourself but seen by others, notably those who recognize the movement because they have a similar beast within themselves. They do not say anything, but they notice and they wonder. No one observes you more shrewdly than someone who is most like you. The style is familiar. This is part of our reality. They sometimes call it the shadow. It does not pay to deny the dark side of the moon, for without the dark side there is no moon.

To my mind, it is contact with this dimension that keeps a person whole. When this side is open there is little danger that one will cultivate delusions about one's self, for one realizes there is no sense in it. Putting a veneer on will not change the inner reality.

The monk, more than any other person, is called upon to open up this aspect of one's being. In fact, the individual's very vocation calls the person to this. For one is called to be a person of prayer, and prayer can take on no serious dimensions until the total individual is involved.

It is not a matter of personal sin, though personal sin is involved and first manifests the presence of evil within. But even when there are still no areas of willful evil, indeed only after the passions have been brought into control and one's moral life brought into order, after years of what can only be called righteous living, does a whole new aspect of the person come to light, and that by hint, by suggestions, by suspicion, by subtle means of one kind or other. Oftentimes it happens by a strange and unmanageable attitude which I cannot account for toward certain people who have habits or leanings or trends or ways that upset me beyond telling. When you put all these together and listen carefully you begin gradually to realize the other side of your being. And this is something to be done with great joy.

This is an odd way to put it, for the matter can be done only with great anguish and in deep faith. It is no fun to learn how poor you really are, unless, of course, this learning is joined to profound faith that truly believes in the love of God and the redemption of man by Jesus Christ. And this is why it is a matter for joy.

It is attaining such realization of God's goodness that opens up life immeasurably. The experience of God's love becomes very real indeed and a great sense of compassion for others begins to grow into significant dimensions. An experience of compassion comes from having drunk deeply of human misery in your own heart. It is no great trick to accept others once you have accepted yourself. But to accept others without having done the same act of mercy to your own self is simply impossible. 'Love your neighbor as yourself', he said.

When, as we say, monastic life is acted out against this total backdrop, then the attitude toward what we call external observances changes radically. It becomes far less frantic, less frenzied, indeed simply less important, for now it can be taken in stride as a kind of play, done seriously and done well, but done with a freedom that gives the whole some sort of joy. That particularly obnoxious quality that tends to surround what we like to call 'pious people' disappears—that dreadful sense of superiority and self-assurance that all the humble talk in the world does not hide. Such people are simply too cocky and too stuck on themselves to live with.

Monks, thank the Lord, are not usually that kind of people. The reasons are not hard to find. They live with one another day and night for years on end, and illusions about one's self are bound to be exposed. Further, contact with reality in prayer, work, service, and one's self opens up the heart. It is good to see what is really going on and to seek to understand it a bit more fully and hasten the process of moving into the depth's of one's own being. This inner exploration has been going on for centuries and westerners have much to learn. The east and many of the ancients were much further along the road than we are. It is particularly interesting to read the Scriptures with these thoughts in mind, for it is positively fascinating to see how many times the actions in Holy Writ are of such a kind as to beckon one to the long journey within.

While not trying to give the impression that such a journey is easy and a matter of routine, I think one must say honestly also that it is not a matter of profound intelligence and great learning. It is primarily a matter of courage and thus related to the Spirit of God given us in baptism and particularly in confirmation, renewed in and intensified in the Eucharist. It also involves a kind of docility, a sense of availability, of dependence and submission that is altogether difficult for persons today, notably westerners who think it is essential to act, to take over, to organize and control everything and above all, to be busy. It is precisely in being still and at peace that we are most effective.

There are things that can help and each must learn to find a way that is suitable to him. No two people are alike and each makes love differently. Some people need physical solitude to feel in any way alone, being much too conscious of the presence of others. Some do not need that sort of thing but, given some quiet, can easily settle into a deep peace. Some need some small thing to do. The rosary used to serve in this manner and for many still does. Formerly much of monastic labor was of this type: humdrum routine tasks that took minimal attention and not too much exertion so that in them one could easily muse, wonder, dwell with something great and wonderful. Psalmody can be like that, even strumming a musical instrument, so long as it be gentle and light, not too professional a sort of thing. Sometimes all people need is the woods, the water, the sky overhead. There is no question at all why so many among the people of God have been shepherds; the idea lends itself perfectly to the creation of a spiritual person.

There is no end of ways, and I have not even mentioned reading! Yet the basic quality must be a kind of restful inner repose, a quiet abiding, a still presence. Not a time for action, for thoughts, for plans, for talking to God or anyone else. It is to be with the one you love and to know that there is no need to do any more than be there. This sounds so simple and easy, so very attractive and obvious, but it is difficult in some ways.

It is inevitable that as the presence is increasingly more truly experienced there is a sharing of secrets and an unveiling of one's being as we come to know one another better. In other words, love gets serious. This is the test. At such times it will take all your nerve to remain still and let it happen to you. On days like that solitude weighs on the heart like lead. Yet when entered into, when embraced, it turns out to be the most strengthening medicine, the most invigorating tonic. To love and to know that one is loved makes the experience of one's poverty some sort of token payment only. And so we begin to be monks.

THE MONASTIC CHOIR AS SONG
AND DANCE ࿐

I HAVE FOUND that my few years among the primitives of stone age
New Guinea have been a great help to me in the monastic life. Perhaps you will permit me to share a few fruits of that experience with
you.

On Christmas Eve we all prostrated here in the Chapter Room in hon-
or of the Nativity of Our Lord. We also prostrate as a community on
Good Friday, so that on the day of his birth and the day of his death we
lie flat upon the earth. We do the same on our day of entry into the
community and again on the occasion of solemn profession. These are
our own days of dying and being born anew. Primitives see a great significance in contact with the earth, more than just an act of humility or
subjection. A mother will always give birth to a child on the ground.
The houses are usually off the earth on stilts, elevated some six or eight
feet. When her time is approaching the mother will have a hut built on
the ground beneath the house and there will give birth to her young
one. When a person is seriously sick and it is thought that death is on
the way, the same thing is done. The sick one will go lie on the ground,
in a little shelter if there be one or even out in the open, but on the
ground. For the ground is seen as contact with the great mother to
whom we shall all return. They do not see this as degrading or even hu-
miliating, but simply as a great joyful truth: the earth is our mother. We
know that Christ also is of the earth, that he sprang from earth as man
through Mary, and that he was buried in the earth in going down into
death, but that he made this glorious and added a new significance and
dimension to earthly life.

But it is especially in primitive dance that a great deal is hidden. The native loves to dance. He feels a great compassion for us of the western world because we do not dance. His sympathy is well placed, for beyond professional groups and a modest revival in folk dancing, the dance among us is generally considered today to be in a degenerate state, a mark of the degeneration of our times. This fact may account for there being so little use made of the dance in a spiritual context. Native people dance as groups, as communities. Everything in village life is connected with the dance. In fact, everything in life becomes significant because of its connection with the dance. They do not see the dance as a change in the routine of daily life. They see the dance as the only reality worth being concerned with. They take the dance very seriously, prepare long for it. They follow the dance ritual most carefully and enter into it with enthusiasm.

The dance involves costume, language, rhythm, song, and meaning. Feathers, dogs' teeth, pigs' teeth, shells, elaborate headdress, paint—all these are the costume. The dances are so old—I suppose a thousand years old—that the language used in the songs is no longer spoken and has become a forgotten language. The rhythm is the beat of the drum, the stamp of the feet, the steps in a circle, in a single line, in a double line. The women do not take an active part but accompany, with the children surrounding the dancers and marking out the rhythm with them. The accompanying song follows the beat of the wooden hand drums. Sometimes a soloist leads and all answer, sometimes there is dialogue, sometimes song in unison. And what is the meaning of the dance? In the dance primitives enter into another life, another time. In the dance they go back to Paradise, to the day when everything was good, when life was pleasant, when there was no misery or woe, when life was all that it was meant to be. They go back to the first people who learned from God how to hunt and how to build a house, how to fish and how to plow the ground, how to take a dog to the bush and run down a wild boar, how to make a bow and arrow and shoot a bird, how to work the sago from the palm and make themselves a meal. And in the dance all these things are acted out in simple pantomime or are sung of in simple tunes repeated over and over. And so in the dance the natives leave this world behind them and touch the real world, enter upon the real life, touch the time before the unknown tragedy that ruined so much of life on earth. And because they do so, the things of the here and the now take on meaning and value. In the dance they contact all who have gone before them, who hunted as they hunt, who fished and plowed gardens and built houses and took women to wife just as they do. They reach back to the very first days. This return to Paradise is a profound thing to primitives and runs deep into their souls.

All this taught me a great deal about the choir and the monastic life, the chant. Choir is primarily song and dance. Song it surely is. It is a formalized dance, a stylized one, quiet and contemplative in character rather than ecstatic. It does not involve a great deal of movement, but there is rhythm nonetheless in a large number of group actions and postures. There is [Latin] the language from another time, from our ancestors. There is also the music from our forebearers, having a peculiárly religious character because of its use for centuries in worship. The whole adds up to a creation of staggering beauty: the cowls, the psalters, the strange melody and awesome chanting back and forth between the two facing choirs, the bowing and rising and sitting and standing. All this makes an impression that is never forgotten.

As it turns out, the choir is not the only monastic dance, for we have numerous processions, and everyone acknowledges that the procession is a form of dance. Actually, almost the only real dance left in the world today is the procession, the parade. Even though this is scarely dance at its highest level, it is still meaningful. There are few who are not moved by a parade, especially if it is well done, for the well-ordered movement of any large group always fascinates. The military is not unaware of this. As monks we have our processions every day to the Chapter Room and in the refectory, to the Church, to the dormitory. Further, the choir motif is carried on in the Chapter Room and in the refectory, since the seating is in the form of choir, so that even in our eating and in our participation in chapter we, in some way, enter into the scheme of dance. Then there are the cloister processions and those we have on All Souls Day and when we bury our dead. Even in going to work a single file procession is prescribed for use when possible. To the routine business of going to work it adds a religious character. All these are procession and admittedly in the dance form and are often accompanied by chant.

.

Some might kneel in the visitors' gallery of our church and tell me afterwards that the monastic choir was the most impressive thing that they had ever seen. I would agree. They might ask me how long this had been going on in this hidden valley, and I would tell them seven times a day for the last hundred years and more. They might then suggest that it would be good if a lot of people knew about it and came here to see it, that it would edify and inspire. Then I would tell them, 'That is not the point. This is not for you. This is not a performance. We are not here to edify. We do not sing only when there is a visitor in the gallery. This is for God and for God alone. If you want to join us in the praise of God you are most welcome, but think of it as something akin to the song of a robin. It has no special use. It is of no great benefit. It is an act of joy. For what point is there to be a robin? And how necessary is he? Or the robin's song in the wood? Or the wood for that matter. And the valley beside the wood. And the river that flows through, what good is it? Or the sea beyond into which it runs? Indeed, the whole of creation? What is it except a song of God's joy, the outpouring of his love?' And that is the point of being a monk. Monastic song and dance are an expression of joy, the outpouring of hearts in love with God.

But there is a further point. In their song the monks contact a great reality. When they enter choir and set out upon the work of God they enter a new world. They are new people. Here they are in a world of no time, here they are with Christ in eternity, where time is not. Here they touch the shores of heaven. They are one with the ages before the Old Testament, one with Abraham, Isaac, and Jacob, one with Moses and Joshua. Through the Red Sea, through the desert, across the Jordan, into exile and back again. They are with John the Baptist, and celebrate the coming of Christ, his life and his dying and rising, his glorious ascent into heaven and the sending of the Spirit. They celebrate his return at the end of time. Into all this the monks enter, in this world of totality, not by the fragile vehicle of an ancient myth, but by their own being sharing the very being of God. And through this contact with this world of God the present world of the here and now takes on meaning and significance. Because they touch the living Christ in their song, the same song transforms everything it lights upon into something eternal.

That is why we are reminded of choir all day long; not only in going to choir often during the day, but even in chapter, even in the refectory, we are as it were in the world of song and dance. The state of sanctifying grace, as the theologian would say. It could be said that this is the greatest thing we do. That the choir is the whole point and meaning of Gethsemani. And yet if you say that you have not said it right. It is rather that the choir says what Gethsemani says. The work of the hands and the prayer of the heart, the silence and the fasting, the virginal life and the solitude and penance, and the Eucharist, they are all part of this. They all fit together and build the contemplative life, the life for God.

To sing and dance, then, is simply to express one's faith, one's hope, one's love. It may be that because it is so poor in love our age does not dance. But the monk does. And further, by song and dance is one with his lover, in reality, not mere memory. We sing to Christ being born and we dance with him. We sing to Christ on the Sea of Galilee and dance with him on the water. We sing to the Lord at the Last Supper and dance with him. We sing to him in his passion and dance with him dying. We sing and dance to his rising and to his ascending into heaven. We sing and dance to the coming of the Spirit and singing and dancing we await the great coming at the end. And because of this song and dance all things have meaning, all things are tied together in Christ, and life has one point, one knot that unites all: Christ and Christ alone.

Mrs [John] Kennedy showed herself a woman of insight and endowed with a sense of the appropriate when she had the high and mighty of the earth walk in procession from the White House to the cathedral behind the body of her husband. This surely was a profoundly moving thing, men walking the dead to the grave with the widow to the sound of wailing bagpipes and the measured beat of the drums of death. This was a procession. This was a dance. At the grave of President Kennedy she had a group of Irish dancers do the ancient graveside dance for the dead. In silence. This too was most significant and meaningful. Here we dance a man to his grave and dance at his grave, dance him into eternity.

In dance we enter into the rhythm of all things. We enter into the rhythm of life and death, of spring and summer, of fall and winter, of the movement of sun and moon, the stars and their dance through the heavens. It is in this entering into the rhythm of all things that we touch the heart of life. We touch not only the rhythm of the waves beating on our shores, the splendid beauty of the trees bowing gracefully before the wind, we touch the very heart of rhythm in the bosom of the Holy Trinity itself. This is the rhythm that John heard when he leaned upon the heart of Christ. This is what the monk senses in dancing and singing. It is to join the dance of the angels before the throne of God.

And we all dance to the rhythm of our heart beat, to our every breath, our every step. We dance to each passing hour whether in a field of corn, doing the wash, cooking the soup or sewing socks. We all dance. The thing is to dance well and make explicit the monastic song and dance of the love that is in us. The choir as we know it may not be essential to monastic life, but love is. The choir is simply an expression of that love, an expression that is ancient and beauteous, most thoroughly in keeping with the deepest religious instincts of humankind.

Primitives in the stone age jungle can teach us a great deal. They know little, after all, but they do have an insight into things, an awareness of where the truth lies. They have caught the rhythm of life and, though they have caught but a part of it, they have caught a great deal. In fact, many Christians who know a great deal about a great many things often do not have the appreciation of the fundamentals that many a primitive has. That is why I think of it as something of a miracle that through some thousand years and more we still have our traditional monastic choir. I believe we shall sing and dance as long as we have the contemplative life. When that is gone we shall no longer have the choir or want it, and we shall look around for something useful to do. When the monks seek God they will find him, and when they find him you need not worry about them singing or dancing. They will sing and dance until they drop, only to carry on in the kingdom of heaven.

Purity of Heart and Reality ॐ

R EALITY CAN BE PERCEIVED in its fulness only when it is perceived
in rapture. Rapture is a quality of the pure in heart. To perceive
reality in its fulness, therefore, we must be pure of heart. But
rapture is also a quality of play, a fruit of play. We may suspect, then,
that in play lies a road to purity of heart. Such is the burden of this talk:
that in play we are schooled in purity of heart, experience rapture, and
perceive the fulness of reality.

This is not, of course, an original theme. [Romano] Guardini, some
thirty years ago, in his famed *Spirit of the Liturgy*, developed the aspect
of the liturgy as play in a beautiful way. In his view one must approach
the liturgy as play if one is to have a valid grasp of it. The same could be
said of the religious life in general and certainly of the contemplative life.

The difficulty is not only, as Guardini mentioned, that people of a
practical bent of mind do not appreciate this, but also, I think, because
play is little known and little understood. Because our culture does not
know how to play we, as a people, are not characterized by purity of
heart. Nonetheless, the instinct to play abides in every person and waits
only to be developed in order to express itself. For the most part, however, this ability lies dormant or stunted and does not often flourish.

One would be hard put to it to discover true play in the classic sense
of the word, in the world that we know. We have elements of play, to
be sure, in our political life, in the arms race, in some aspects of com-
petitive business, in the endeavor to be first to the moon. There is some
small amount of play in our frenzied cult of sport and games. There is
also a bit in the impassioned pursuit of fun and pleasure. But in all these
instances the quality of play is not developed to anything near its capacity and, further, what element is there is invariably vitiated by selfishness,

by desire for gain, by hatred, by uninhibited sensuous excess. We are a people of pleasure and fun, seeking good times, recreation, diversion, activities to fill our leisure and to distract us. But we are not a people that plays. The reason for this is simple enough: none of our so-called play has a spiritual quality.

Play in the classic sense must include an element of the spiritual, of the rapturous, the ecstatic. This is the universal human experience. In this area, as in others, we as a people are simply not normal. That being so, we can understand the particular problems we experience in the endeavor to attain purity of heart. Play in the classic sense includes many factors, among them: order, beauty, rhythm, tending, struggle or striving, movement, rapture. Play is out of the realm of ordinary life, in a special place, a special time. Play is extremely serious. Those who participate must be unselfish. Play serves no special usefulness or purpose. All these characteristics are involved in real play, noble play, play in the classic sense. Play is not acting, but a mode of action; not pretending, but a protection from pretense; not work, but a background for work; not life, but a way of living, a form or style of being, a natural setting for a supernatural life.

It might well be questioned at this juncture: if classic play is not known among us, if play is not understood, then why bother with it? You will only confuse and distress and upset people. I think, however, that the matter is worth mention if for no other reason than to point up the fact that the world from which we come, the society we have grown up with, the culture of which we are a product as well as an agent, is not a normal and healthy one. It suffers grievous drawbacks of a very serious kind. One of them is a lack of real play. This being so inevitably causes us difficulty in adjusting to anything as healthy and normal as the religious life which, as I see it, cannot possibly be understood in the right sense if one has no sense of play.

In our culture we are taught to do most things for rather selfish reasons. We seek ourselves in everything, we go to work to earn money to buy the things we want. We go to school in order to get better work where we may make more money in less time with less effort. We play games for the pleasure of it. We seek amusement for fun to the point of this being almost a national obsession. This selfish spirit touches all life:

the life of learning, of work, of pleasure, even of religion. Because we unconsciously seek ourselves in almost all we do, when we turn to religion, we are apt to be rather selfish. We seek the pleasure of being good, or of being thought good. We seek to become perfect so that we may enjoy the composure that comes of doing well. We may enter the religious life and there seek our own happiness, measuring the value of the life and our place in it by how happy we are. We may keep the rule perfectly, make a life work of it because we then feel better. We may handle the religious life as we would any human enterprise: building a bridge or selling insurance or driving a bus . . . as a production of our own, pursued for our own purposes. In the case of religion we do this ultimately for God, of course, and indeed with God, in the grace of God, but beneath it all the whole may be marred by a kind of selfishness that one is hardly aware of. The heart is not pure.

When a brother walks from the cloister to the dairy barn, what is the reality involved? I might say, a person has decided to go from one place to another and sets in motion everything required to achieve that. That is all? Well, there is more involved, if you press the point, since this individual is a monk and all he does has a particular beauty and significance, is marked by the immolation of the vows, by his life in obedience. That being so, walking to the dairy barn is especially pleasing to God. That is all.

But there is more. Is not this person, as human being, one with Abraham called on a journey by God? Is he not one with the Jews delivered from Egypt, led through the Red Sea, across the desert? Is not every step taken a step with the chosen people of God, with them through the Jordan and into the Promised Land? Is he not one with Christ on his way to Jerusalem, indeed one with him on his journey from the heavenly Father to us and then back again? And in that journey linked with all humanity—past, present and to come? Does not walking to the dairy barn say all that? Indeed it does, for the reality is not that this person is moving from here to there. The reality is that one is on the way to eternity. Every breath drawn, every step taken, every moment of time brings it closer. That the monk will ever reach the dairy barn is in question. He may change his mind. But there is no question about attaining to eternity. That is inevitable. He will not change his mind about that. The reality of this walk to the dairy barn involves this whole picture. What we see with the senses, photograph with the camera, define with our limited scale of human measure, is mere skim on the surface of reality.

If this be true of going to the dairy barn, then must not the same be said no matter where one goes or what one is doing within the orbit of one's life for God? Is not all one does a great deal more than it appears to be? Then is it not all play? So as simple a thing as getting up in the morning is not then just a matter of a monk getting out of bed to begin another day. Indeed not. Another day is a new creation. We are in a new day fresh from the hands of God. I have risen from the tomb of my bed, from the death of my sleep. The world is in a time that is a new time, a virginal time that never was before and is created and given me now. The world is all new. This great universe is where it never was before, for we have all sped through space to a new day, both a new time and a new place. Today is lone, unique, solitary. I stand alone before my Creator as at the dawn of the first day. One with Adam, I lift my head to God for joy. One with Christ, I come forth to do the Father's will. I put on my socks, my shoes, and go forth on the ways of my Lord and Brother.

And what is a procession in the cloister but play? We put on our cowls and cloaks, we walk in double file, following the cross, accompanied by the Abbot, singing songs, with candles and clouds of incense. What is this but play for God? It has no other purpose but pure joy in God, as pure as the song of a bird, the blooming of a rose, the splendor of a blue sky. It is but to walk with Christ and with my friends on our way together into eternity.

It is through the symbolic aspects of our life that we are continually brought into touch with the great realities that surround us. For there is no need always to be imagining the spiritual relation of all that we are doing. This would take too much energy. But by symbol we are now and again reminded of the great realities that surround us. And this is enough to give us our bearings. Just as we are in Kentucky and never really forget it, or are in America and are never quite out of touch with this reality even though not always conscious of it in a specific way, so too, in the liturgy, in symbols, we have brought to our minds the great reality just outside the scope of our senses. In viewing the religious life under this aspect of holy play we are helped to enter into the life freely and with that total abandon necessary if we are to attain purity of heart. It must be stressed how great is the necessity of a genuine entering into all we do, into prayer and reading, into silence and solitude, into simplicity and penance and denial. We cannot enter into the greater reality without first entering the lesser. It is precisely selfishness that can make this very difficult. We tend to build a life on our own terms, after our own specifications, well meant, perhaps, but bound to end in futility because it is rooted in selfishness. You cannot play sort-of, kind-of. It is through a grasp of the life as a kind of holy playing in which we give ourselves without holding back that we perhaps have a genuine approach, at least one that is deeply in sympathy with human nature. Then we can enter into the rapture that is part of all play and a necessary component of the contemplative life, fruit of purity of heart, and obviously, of humility, characteristic of the ingenuousness of the child. A false concept of play is not unknown, and sometimes souls who have insight into things will realize that play is in some way involved in the life, but misinterpret this to mean that nothing is to be taken seriously, that we play *at* the life, that we do not really pray, do not really work, do not really keep silent or bear pain or accept suffering and anguish, do not do anything with ardor or enthusiasm. Even children will be quick to point out the flaw in this and will tell you to your face that you 'don't get into it'. This is a vicious business and makes progress in the life impossible. It is the fruit of cowardice, that is to say, pride, and the refusal to take play seriously.

We have come apart to this place called Gethsemani, have come behind these walls, are established within this enclosure, this sacred ground. Here we are together. We have a common father, a common rule. We have things to do. What are these things? We pray, we read, we work, we eat, we sleep. The rule or the abbot tells us which to do and when, where and how to do it. The rule or the abbot decides the clothes we wear, the food we eat, the songs we sing. And the life is silent, simple, solitary, and secluded.

Here you have all the elements of classic play: order, beauty, place, rhythm, solemnity, movement, striving, repeating, and one more quality, the joy of rapture, the ecstasy of possession. This is the greatest quality of play, its most significant aspect. For in play we get out of ourselves, we leave our small world of here and now, the world of the senses, the world I see and taste and touch and feel, the world that appears to be reality and is not, which poses as reality but is only a poor approximation of it. In play I enter into the whole of reality. My spirit can touch the infinite, and unless a person's life has windows that open on the infinite one will go mad. Half the madness in our mad age must be derived from humanity's present lack of that noble play by which people come into contact with the eternal world of which they are a part.

Whence came the only spiritual music of any significance that this land has produced to date? Whence came the most beautiful of our folk songs? You know as well as I do. They have come from the play of Negro slaves doing wretched hard labor and transforming it into a spiritual significance, accompanying it with music and song that no one who has ever heard has been able to forget. This is perhaps one of the finest examples of spiritual play that our land has known. The Negro spirituals are every bit as profound as the Psalms and are their cousins.

Why did I find [when I was in 'the world'] that in suburban u.s.a. the people, though of great faith, entered into the liturgy very little indeed, in an apathetic way, while in primitive New Guinea there was enthusiastic participation? It cannot be said that the Roman liturgy is more kin to Melanesia than to mid-America! I think the reason is not so much in the structure of the liturgy as in the ability to play. We do not know how to play; primitives do. Is it not possible that some of our difficulties with liturgy, usages, customs, derive not so much from weakness in the forms of our life as much as weakness in ourselves? This is certainly not beyond question. It is not just a matter of language, that is sure.

In the morning, then, I rise with Christ, and with Christ I go to pray and with Christ I chant the office and with Christ I break my fast with bread and coffee. With Christ I commune in secret prayer in my heart, with Christ I read the Good Book, go to work. With Christ I love my brother and bear the heat and suffer pain and know heartache, endure loneliness, and keep silent, suffer rebuke and quench anger. With Christ I walk the earth and count the stars at night. The same sun as shone on him shines on me. The moon that lighted his Gethsemane lights mine.

The same rain that fell on his holy head falls on mine, runs down my neck. I walk the earth he walked, live the life he lived.

If these things happen to me in Christ and I do these things in Christ, then I do them with the whole human family. For with every person who ever lived I lie down each night and sleep. I rise in the morning. I work. I pray. I read. I suffer. With all of humanity, past, present and to come. In Christ. That being so, I share in some way with the total life of the whole earth, of the whole universe. I touch eternity and eternal life in God by the trivial things I do every day, in every breath I draw, every time I take a drink of water.

That is the rapture I enter into in my play. This is the point and the purpose of the game we enter into. It is not just to enjoy myself or have fun, not even to find myself or become an integrated personality or find happiness. Rather, it is to enter into reality, to find the truth, to see God, and to attain that in purity of heart.

When we approach reality with pure hearts and in the humble spirit of children we shall not only seek God but find him. It is not so difficult. The instinct to play is God-given and lives in every human heart. Children play naturally all over the world. The natural play of childhood should accompany us into maturity and there grow in stature and mystical significance. The pity is that this instinct gets trampled on very early in life, and in a culture like ours is sometimes nearly smothered. But it can be revived, be developed. One must start with reality. We have to play, first of all. We cannot break the rules, cannot cheat. We cannot stand on the side and watch. We cannot be show-offs, prima-donnas. Nor can we get mad, pick up our marbles and go home, literally or figuratively. We have to give it all we've got, or try to. And be good losers, too. We cannot mope or drag our feet or whine or grumble or complain all the time. These rules we all know; we learned them as kids.

So we have to get into it, have to see that playing is the thing. It is not important how we feel or what we like or what we want. It is not important whether we shine or not, whether we succeed or not, whether we especially like what we do or not. To do other than that is simply to be selfish and not to see that it is all play. By playing, in faith, we see that the real significance of things is hidden and no less real for all that. It is whole-hearted commitment which is marked by no selfish angles that is the sign of perfection in the art of living for God, the sign of purity of heart. Those who are not so pure are either not committed or they have an angle.

Christ complained of those who would not play with him. We have piped, he said, and you have not danced. We have sung dirges and you have not mourned. He says as much to us. Play along with me. Suffer as I did. Sweat as I did. Bear pain as I did. Work and toil as I did. Bear failure and misunderstanding as I did. Die as I did.

To do this, to know this, is the key to joy, for you cannot touch the joy of one who has been united to Christ. There is nothing you can do to rob a person of this joy, absolutely nothing. One's delight is to be with the Lord, playing with him at all times, playing in the world. Blessed are the pure in heart, who have become as little children, for they shall see God in all things.

I sat on the hill and watched a Brother slowly going up and down the bottom with the tractor, seeding corn. It was as beautiful a morning as God had ever made. Above me in the trees seven birds were singing in wild abandon, for sheer joy. Beside me in the fenced-in meadow two brown horses were racing back and forth up to their knees in wet grass, kicking and frolicking. The clouds above were massive white and gold with purple eye shadow. A light breeze was blowing in from the east, moving the light mist ever so gently, for the cool hollows were shrouded in fog. Who was playing most or best? The horses in the dewy field, the birds in the sycamores, the clouds in the sky? The Brother who had gone forth to sow his seed? Or God in his heaven? It does not matter, for all were playing, each in his own way, and a great joy was shared by heaven and earth. I went to sing Prime. I thought the pitch high and the choir flat and I was mad. But that did not matter either. I was singing with the angels. That was real, singing with Christ in his glory, singing with everyone on the earth, with the Brother on the tractor, with the Brother dying in the infirmary, with every person on earth: the good and the bad, the virtuous and the dissolute, the sober and the drunken, the free and the imprisoned, the rich and the poor, people dying and leaving the world, people being born and just coming into it. I sing with them all in Christ.

If this is not perfect joy there is none. What matter if my own heart be barren and empty, my mind a sterile waste, my own life full of fuss and fury. It does not matter. You do not have to be holy to love God. You have only to be human. Nor do you have to be holy to see God in all things. You have only to play as a child with an unselfish heart, and so be lost in rapture at the great reality that lies hidden just under the surface of everything.

THE PLAGUE ⳥

I N HIS NOVEL *The Plague* Camus describes a modest city in Algeria
which is overtaken by the plague and for most of a year suffers grie-
vously under it, being meanwhile shut off from all contact with the
outside world. It is a story magnificently told and of profound significance. No monk could read it without sensing the overtones that come
through to him clearly and touch on many aspects of his life. Whether
Camus was a Christian or not and whether he wrote from a Christian or
deliberately non-christian point of view is not really the point. He described a human situation in depth and therefore he necessarily is involved with something no Christian can dismiss.

One does not often read a story with the impact that Camus achieves
in this description of what happens to a city and its people when struck
down by something they can do nothing about. The most terrifying aspect of it is the fact that the problem arose from within. In truth the
plague rose from their own depths, since out of their own cellars and
sewers and dumps hundreds and then thousands of rats appeared in the
open only to die in writhing agony while spewing blood. This event did
not escape the inhabitants and bothered them no little bit, for everyone
knew that the rats arising out of the cellars of Oran to die in full view of
the citizenry were really no more than the long repressed and hidden aspects of their own lives, hidden away so subtly and completely as to be
entirely forgotten, leaving the inhabitants to live only on the surface in a
manner wholly artificial. It is not only that rats live in cellars; it is the
rats which first appear when one loses contact with one's inner depths.

It is not long before the fleas on the plague-stricken rats carry the disease to the people. In short order the plague is raging in the city and
deaths mount from a few a day into a few hundred despite all efforts to

stop it. The story is concerned with the reactions of representative characters to this situation, from doctor to artist to thief to priest to police to fathers and mothers and children and tavern keepers and mixed-up people.

It does not take much imagination to see how this ties in with the monastic situation. In the monastery we have a representative group of people confined for a prolonged period and exposed to infection. What is the infection they are exposed to? Themselves, as manifest in their own lives and in the lives of those around them. What often escapes us as a most significant aspect of monastic living is that there is no escape. We are confined here under relatively severe control and exposed to the vision both of ourselves as we are and of each other. For all practical purposes we might just as well walk about perfectly nude when it comes to the extent of our exposure to one another. Here no one hides anything. I see you as you are and you me. For one cannot live elbow to elbow with others day in and day out, at work as well as at prayer, coming and going, good days and bad, summer and winter, year in and year out, without coming to know them fairly well. Not totally perhaps, but fairly well.

This is one of the basic components of the monastic experience, not the specifics of the enclosure which vary from time to time and from one century to another, but the peculiar dimension given life when you look at it for a long time without distraction and diversion. What do you see when you really look at a person? What happens when one is not protected by a front or a set of devices or a mask or a costume one puts on and takes off at will for the benefit of those contacted for short intervals. What happens when one no longer bothers about masks and fronts and appearances?

Further, what happens when one is content not merely to look on one's neighbor as a strange freak, but comes to see one's self as one sees the neighbor, in terms fairly close to the truth. Or better, when listening to the depths within, one comes to hear things that are not expected or to detect rising from within strange visions and peculiar dreams? This is when the life begins to get a bit rough. You begin to discern that what is wrong with other people is you or that the glaring disaster in someone else's makeup is but a reflection of the same within yourself? Or worse yet, what if the rats begin to crawl out of your own cellar? Ah, we are now close to panic, for we see that these rats carry with them a loathsome disease that strikes down both us and others.

This is the situation that Camus described in *The Plague*. The various responses of the people of Oran in the face of this disaster were a summary of the reaction of one who comes to discover one's own genuine dimensions. In other words, we are concerned with the problem of evil in its deepest aspect. And here again, we move a step beyond personal sin, guilt, fault, onto another plane of the realms of darkness, what we might call evil influences, forces, powers. How are you going to explain this? Having come to know these powers within, what are you going to do?

Camus faced this problem in his novel. We ought not to find fault with his response if we ourselves have no response at all or, worse yet, have not even come to meet these forces of evil within. Most of the people of Oran were outraged at the onslaught of the disease in their midst as something totally unwarranted and undeserved. They saw no reason why they should have been chosen for an outbreak of this hideous, death-bringing monster.

The monk, it would seem to me, has not merely admitted that such a plague is already present in all of us. He goes one step further and takes definite steps to do something about it. Or, to put it differently, the doctrine of original sin suddenly comes to life and is discovered as a living reality within one. We discover that there are dimensions of evil within quite apart from one's history of personal sin. Even after habits of serious sin have gone, if they were ever present, there remains a kind of innate direction toward evil which we identify under the general heading of original sin and its effects.

The monk's response to this situation is not denial nor is it refuge in the fact that humanity is also good, that if it has its dark side, it has also its bright, that if we suppress the one we work to cultivate the other. This is well and good, but as the monk also knows, not enough. There is something else yet, some way of going beyond both good and evil into something further in, beyond immediate experience.

We begin, in short, to enter into the realms where dwells the secret of our true identity, where the true person lies hidden, wrapped in some mysterious divine presence which dwells within and which is brought into an expression of its full beauty in the grace given us. The priest, Paneloux, on the one hand and the doctor, Rieux, on the other take opposite views: one sees in the plague just punishment for sin, the other simply an enemy to be fought by any and every means possible. If both are right, and in a sense they are, both are wrong, too, in that they do not pursue the matter to its ultimate meaning, that human dignity and beauty lie beyond the good and evil in a person, and that the grace of God is given not so much to adorn humanity as to restore it to its original stature, to rekindle within that divine fire which was its in the beginning.

The monk in his monastery, like the citizen of Oran confined within quarantine, is able to look reality full in the face and to reckon that disease and suffering are as much a part of contemporary human life as are virtue and goodness. This does not condemn or justify anyone. A person's significance lies in having been created by God. This significance remains. When it is illumined and enkindled by the light of grace one sees beauty for what it truly is, reckons one's self among the sons of God and children of the kingdom.

The way to this true experience of our being is Christ. It is through him that we pass through suffering, death, are plunged into the realms of the underworld and rise into the manhood for which we were created. In him we can make this journey, without him we cannot.

Thus, we must be deceived neither by the good of humanity nor by its evil. The good people are capable of in knowledge, achievement, and mastery of this world leads us to suspect that they are almost divine. The evil that they are capable of and subject to—war, famine, disease, sorrow, death, murder, hatred—lead us to surrender all hope and conclude that they are diabolical. Humanity is neither God nor Satan. It is indeed godlike, but it has been touched by the evil one. But the godliness that is ours cannot lead us astray and have us drive the evil in us underground and out of sight, for as certain as we live, it will not remain there. On the other hand, we are not wholly evil, nor can we succumb to the satanic influence in our own lives or the lives of others under the conviction that humanity is wholly dissolute, corrupt, and lost.

We are now living in an era in which it comes home to us in greater and greater measure that the dream of our own goodness is an illusion of the worst sort. Now we witness the plague that has broken out in our midst, brought to us by the rats out of our own cellars, that is to say, coming from our own unacknowledged depths. The hatred, wrath, violence, and fury of our times, the unparalleled evil manifest in war and mass murder has never seen its equal in history. Yet we only admit in the mildest of mild voices that perhaps there may be something wrong and set to work with a vengeance to prove how good we really are. And like so many distraught passengers on a rocking vessel, we move frantically from one side to the other, with each succeeding rush bringing the ship ever closer to total disaster.

The monk is neither one to deny human goodness nor is he one to sit and grovel in the pool of human misery, insisting in the face of all worldly lords that people are corrupt and lost. He rather reckons that both are part of the total scene, that we have good in us and bad. We can drive neither the one nor the other out. We must take both in hand, acknowledging at once our almost infinite capacity as immortal children of the heavenly Father and keeping well in mind also that there is no evil we are not capable of.

All of which is well and good and no great problem so long as it is kept in the abstract. As long as we deal in generalities all is well. It is only when we get specific that the problems begin, for it is my wife who is dying and my brother who was killed in Vietnam and my daughter who has cancer. Then all theories sound weak. All talk of good and evil sounds like just that: talk.

With that no one would argue.

There is no person who can answer the problem of evil, which is another way of saying that we have need of Christ. It is in him that we make our way to the Father, through him that we have an understanding of the human passion. It is in his spirit and in the light of his grace that we pass through the darkness of this world, not by understanding everything, but by faith.

In Jesus Christ a person is restored to one's primal beauty and holiness, enabled once more to walk erect and to set the heart on the kingdom for which one was created, strengthened meanwhile to recreate the earth in the same power and grace that recreated the individual that in so doing the kingdom may be forwarded.

The most disturbing truth about the people of Oran and their reaction to the plague was this: they liked it; in their heart of hearts they liked it. They welcomed it. They were glad for it. They did almost nothing about it until they had no choice, and, as long as they could they permitted it to be, ignored it and secretly wished it well. But this they never would have admitted. There is a profound truth here and one would do well to consider, not so much as musing on a French novel, but as some quiet thoughts on our own condition.

Perhaps you have noticed this in yourself? Seeing a disaster about to take place, you hoped it would? This is an aspect of the same mystery. This need not be wilful, of course, but a simple prime reaction that is almost unconscious, but illuminating.

Many people are glad for the disasters that overwhelm them, are pleased at the suffering they must undergo. Many even help the cause along. This is considerably more than mere love for penance and denial. Nor is it only a hope of participating in the passion of Christ and so working with him for the salvation of humanity. It is not nearly so refined as that, not so developed. It is basically a kind of hatred for life. The monk becomes aware of this possibility within, for one does not have to be a monk to know that many accidents may be deliberate.

What led the people to love the plague even though they hated it? Why do people punish themselves? Whence the power of this strange hatred that turns the weapon on one's self? What else except the embrace of the evil that one has driven out? The seven devils come back to the room swept and garnished, and are welcomed by the inhabitants of the house. This is as good a test as any of our contact with evil in us, of our mastery of it, and of our love for Christ

If we cannot use the good in us as a measure of praise for ourselves, so we cannot hate another because of the evil in the person. Humanity is not lovable because it is good nor hateful because it is evil. It is lovable because it is made by God and worthy of dignity, reverence, and respect in its own right. Unless we perceive this truth in full measure we run the risk of surrender to hatred not only for others but primarily for ourselves. This is to base our regard for the human person not on intrinsic value but on appearances. One is worthy of love whether good or evil. And so are you.

This is impossible to do without Christ. We forever tend to value ourselves for our own goodness, and in order to do so we crush the evil in us, casting it from our sight. But this never works, for then the evil comes out in others or is driven into our own depths, only to come out later in some form or other of hatred. No, we must be able to go beyond good and evil, even in ourselves.

The monk in the monastery soon comes to discover these truths and to experience them and continues to do so all his days as a monk. He is busy in the beginning acquiring a certain monastic goodness, which is only right and decent. But not long afterwards the aspect of evil begins to enter in and clouds everything up and makes the happy life confused and disturbed. A kind of plague breaks out in the heart as one discovers aspects of one's reality that are highly disconcerting. Then comes an acceptance of the situation in Christ and an awareness that evil is part of life, that darkness is companion to light, that shadow is the other side of brightness. So a kind of peace is established in which one knows both sides of one's nature in significant depth. And having come so far, one pauses.

The breakthrough is yet to come. It is possible only if one has come to terms with both the evil and the good in oneself, ready as much to acknowledge the one as the other. There is no question that the monastic *ascesis* is of paramount importance in this, since life together with its inbuilt factors of service, patience, and tolerance opens up the inner realities. With Christ among his own as well as with him in solitude, the monk comes to grasp in some way total reality until bit by bit one moves beyond into the inner realm where the true person dwells, where God is enthroned in light and where one's name is written, never to be blotted out for all eternity.

Here one comes to perceive the magnificence of life and its eternal glory, and here and here alone die all tendencies to root one's worth in the good one does or to condemn one's self in hatred for the evil one experiences within. This is to move beyond good and evil into the realms of light.

Here, in contact with one's deepest self, one is at once in contact also with others and with God, for our being is grounded in His. That is why the monk plays so valid a role in the world, for in discovering what the human condition is, he awakens persons to their own dignity and touches them where they are most sensitive to touch, in their being.

In a world which is truly plague-ridden there is no greater thing to do than to embrace the sublime reality which is humanity and to love it with an impassioned love in Christ, far beyond its goodness or its badness. This is the only cure and the only healing and it is the curing and the healing that is ours in Christ and in him alone, he who walked the ways of light and darkness, of death and of hell, and rose that we might follow after him as becomes the children of God.

The Lady of Gethsemani ❧

I HAVE BEEN WONDERING these last several weeks as to the mode and the manner of the presence of the Mother of God among us. I do not mean in imagery only: in the old abbey window we used to have, in the German wooden statue of the cloister, in the picture of her appearance at Guadalupe which we celebrate next Monday, in the rather sleek interpretation in white marble in the woods out back, in the tapestry for the new church. I mean something more than that. More than by imagery, by shrines, more even than by prayer and invocation in the *Salve Regina* each evening, in the antiphons of the Circumcision which we repeat before each hour of the office, in our calling this abbey after her. I mean more than our own private homage to Our Lady. I mean her special presence in this place.

How is she here? How do I know she is here? I know she is not, as they say, substantially present, present as Christ is present. Yet she is here in some way, part of this place in more than it just being named for her, or even that her name is much spoken here.

There are symbols, of course. The lovely blue haze that is so much a part of our landscape is surely a sign of her. The sweet earth of spring, the gentle rain, the air we breathe, the wind. Every flower, every harvest of corn, of wheat, of fruit, is a sign of her fruitful womb. But what I mean is, where is she in you? How do I know she is part of your life, of your spirit? For she is here. That I know. How do I know?

I

I will tell you. Something happened here that gave me as much joy as a good dinner, the plans of Mr Schickel for the new church, or the poetry of Bob Dylan. More joy still, since these are things that happened to us. I am thinking of something that happened from us. It was so humble that I am almost ashamed to mention it, so lowly that it seems almost inappropriate in so solemn an assembly. But I will tell you because one can give no more than what one has.

Just before the last group left for Chile* a dog wandered into Gethsemani. You never saw such a dog. Dirty, hungry, skinny, with a big chunk chewed out of one ear, a hobbling limp from a broken rear leg, and worst of all a cringing, frightened look that told you one thing very clearly: this dog had been beaten often and long and brutally. You could not get near her at first for her fear. And if you did succeed she at once cowered on the ground and rolled over, indicating that she had been beaten often enough on the back. She was a pathetic sight.

Well, you know the rest. Now this monk and now that talked to her, patted her, whistled to her. Got a little food someplace. Some bones, some scraps of meat. And bit by bit she got whole, put on a little weight. Began to look alive. And you could sometimes get close to her. But it took time. When she ate she would gulp down the food as if it were stolen or forbidden; preferred to eat alone and not observed. And sometimes when you put your hand out to her quickly she would cringe and pull back. Still, bit by bit she got better. She started to play and run, limp notwithstanding. She even barked now and then, began to love life again.

Well, dogs and monasteries somehow do not always get along well. One day they thought that perhaps the most prudent thing to do would be to take the dog to Bardstown and find her a home. The next day the dog came back, walking fourteen miles. They did that a couple of more times, and each time she came back a few days later. She is still here. Yesterday she was out back bravely barking at her own echo across the valley.

I am not recommending that we set up a compound for all lost and strayed dogs. I know well enough that this dog and the monastic way of life may not remain long compatible. I am not interested in that. In any case, the dog's days are numbered one way or the other. And there are

*to found there the Monastery of La Dehesa

millions of dogs. Millions. And more hungry people around than dogs who can use love and care, not to say food, better than dogs can. And I am quite aware that you can get sentimental about dogs and cats and tell stories of people who leave fortunes of good American money for foundations to take care of cats while humans go hungry.

But I am not arguing that. I am just saying that a stray dog wandered in here looking for love and got it. And that is what makes me glad. Glad, because to me that is the sign of the woman. And the woman is the Mother of God. Any woman would give a dog something to eat. Find a warm place for it. Show it a little love. For a while anyway. There are no women here. But there is one woman here whom no one sees. Her presence is powerful among us. I know it. The marks of her presence are tenderness, kindness, pity, a reverence for living things, an ability to see God in all things made. It is the Mother of God and her presence among us that make these factors strong. And there is much of this here. The stray dog who wandered in simply manifested it, was a sign sent by God. This poor dumb creature knew the presence of love instinctively and came back to it again and again. I know we have love for God and we have love for one another, and I am not really worried about that. But when you see love for poor dumb things then you are sure that there is truly love for God and man. And I have seen it often. I have seen the monks in tender care for horses and cows, especially when sick. With goats. With birds. Do you want to know about people? Don't ask how much money they have. Find out how they treat their dogs. That's the way they will treat you in the end.

I have seen lots of poverty. I was brought up in the depression. Much poverty embitters, hardens. You have to be real careful with poverty: it will bounce. It boomerangs. I have known religious and priests too who were poor, real poor. But hard also. And mean. Poverty made them that way. Much poverty is an expression of hatred, not of love. I know. I have seen it. Not that wealth is any safer. Wealth can make you haughty and proud and arrogant. Many wealthy people are like that. Priests and religious too. But not all. Nor are all people hard and bitter. But my point is that being poor of itself is no great thing unless it is something of the heart. And even having many possessions in itself is no great thing, one way or the other. Let me see your heart. Let me hear it beat.

And that is why I was so glad for a dog that wandered in. She got exactly what you would think she would get from a monastery, and she got it in rich measure: tender love.

I have heard it said that there is no love around here, but I do not believe it. And I can prove it is wrong. I will show you a dog named Limp.

If people dedicated to God and the things of God, people of prayer and penance and work, people of denial, of obedience, of purity and fasting and vigil and silence—if such people are so tenderhearted as to fuss over a wandering dog, then God be praised in his heaven because his mother is present on earth. For a woman loves life and all living things. And so must anyone who will be whole, complete. A person is not head only. There must also be heart. If you are strong but not gentle, then you are not strong at all, but weak. If you are tough but not kind, then you are not tough at all, but weak. It is the Mother of God who will teach us these things in her presence among us. It is this love among ourselves that gives God glory and us joy. For is not each one of us in some way just like that wandering dog? Have we not been bruised and beaten by life? Been chewed up? Knocked around? Do we not all limp one way or other? Is there any one here bold enough, foolish enough to maintain that he or she is sound? Whole and perfect? Has not the evil one rather left his mark on us all? And is not our gravest problem the fact that we do not believe in love, that we are suspicious and afraid, do not trust? That when God himself comes close we cower for fear of him, having been beaten down once before by one stronger than ourselves? And do we not have the same desire to live? That want for affection and love, that need for nourishment and fulfillment? Do we not seek just as much to be free and to take delight in the world God made, here and to come?

II

And now we come close to another mystery. For the poor dog is touched further with the power of the evil one, the evil one brought into the world by sin, who tainted thereby all creation. For the dog is not content to run the fields and woods for joy, but seeks out some witless rabbit to kill, or worse, stalks down some grace-filled deer and runs it to death over a barbed-wire fence, only to hack it until the blood runs and then walk off leave the carcass to the wild birds. Why is that? Why is darkness part of light? And death part of life, pain the companion of bliss?

This we learn from the Mother of God: to love life, to believe in love, and to enter into darkness. To look on pain, to bear suffering, to live with failure, not with bitterness, but with hope. Not with rancor and revenge, but with faith in the ultimate victory of good. A person is a wandering dog, beaten up, hungry, lost, looking for a little love. And when love comes, one is afraid. One doubts. So everyone needs Mary's touch. Her gentle hand, her quiet way, her benign presence. And she is here. In this house. On our land. In our hearts. Watch her. Listen to her. Abide with her. Say nothing. Do nothing. Just let her be around you. After a while your fever will cool, your bitterness soften, your fears be resolved, your courage restored. And then you will be able to accept the world, be open to it, tolerant of it.

The woman who is Mary was mother to a murdered Son. You cannot live half a life and so you have to live it all. The Mother of God shows us how. So long as there be any meanness in us toward any of God's creatures, human or beast, we must hasten to the Mother of God.

So when a dog wandered in here a few months ago, looking for love and finding it, you may be sure my heart was glad for it. For it means that the Mother of God is among us, in image and song and name and reality. And I can think of nothing that the world needs more than the presence of the Mother of God.

III

You understand, of course, that this simple dog story is an allegory. More than poor dogs come to our gate. People come. Poor people. In an endless stream. Looking for what? God only knows. Looking for gas, for bread, for clothes, for shoes, for peace, for a few days of quiet, for inspiration and counsel, for prayer, but mostly for love.

And they find it. Even those who come here because they would like to share the life of the monk by living it. Some of them are pretty sad. Like the twenty-two year old lad who walked from Washington, D.C., or the man who lived on one hamburger a day, or the big Irish kid from

Chicago who practically forced his mother to drive him down here. Obviously, he was not quite right, but quite loveable. He would not leave the place and wandered all over house and land and woods and finally had to be found by the police. How he loved the monks. When he got home he talked of nothing else. He voluntarily submitted to the needed medical care and set to work on a book about God and love and the monks of Gethsemani.

We see this constant stream of the hungry, the poor, the lonely, the heartsick, the headsick, the weary, the struggling and the failing, the successful, the prosperous, the young and old. What do they all express except the search for God that is our own life. For truly they are scarcely different from any of us, save in a degree or two to the left or to the right.

And we who portray the mystery of the search for God, what are we if not the symbol of the love of God which drew us here in the first place? For we would not be here had not love drawn us.

We are ourselves, then, the poor knocking on our own gate, the hungry looking for a bit of bread, a dog looking for a little love. We are seeking tender love, that of the lady who lives here, whose house this is, the Lady of Gethsemani.

May she pardon me for speaking so ineptly of her.

Searching for the Heart ❧

WHEN IT COMES to a question of the merit or the value of some monastic practices, the greatest concern generally seems to lie in the area of simplicity, and close to that may run a quest for meaning. These are, I realize, loose terms and vague concepts, but I think they do in some way represent an overall frame of mind. I am not too sure it is a good frame, nor do I wholly subscribe to it.

I find particularly disturbing the effort made to create the impression that monastic life and its liturgy are genuine, or more likely to be so, when they are modest, very simple, austere, and even primitive. And secondly, that we are closest to our best Cistercian traditions when this condition prevails. I wonder about these views, or various shades of them.

I submit, first of all, that the Cistercian tradition is not one of very primitive settings for the monastic life, for no matter what Citeaux originally looked like, it did not long remain in that condition. Further, while there can be no doubt that some kind of monastic life can be had with a small and intimate group living in rugged conditions, I do not accept as proven that this is the best, the ideal, the Cistercian way, or, finally, the one most suited for our times.

On the contrary, I would maintain, on the basis of history and experience, that the facilities necessary for the monastic life in some depth are considerable and are best provided for when the group is relatively large. A certain amount of chaste splendor, of *élan*, of dimension, of size, is necessary before liturgical action can have much impact in the monastic setting, both in reference to the size of the church and the number taking part. And to my mind, the authentic Cistercian tradition lives not in a shanty or a hay loft with a handful of monks bravely trying to manage somehow, but rather in a handsome church with full choir characterized by a pure and noble beauty of service.

This kind of appeal to tradition is indeed dangerous, since Cistercian history is so long and so varied that almost any interpretation of our life can be justified by someone, anything from having palatial abbatial quarters to acquiring vast holdings of land and cornering the European wool market. This cannot be denied. On the other hand, again with a call to tradition and the sources, there is a somewhat wistful hankering for the primaeval swamp and the rugged challenge of the first Citeaux, however transient that stage may have been. All this notwithstanding, I believe there can be found in much of the history of the Order a persistent orientation around a liturgy, as well as a whole monastic life, which is characterized by austere dignity, noble and simple beauty; which, while admittedly hard to make explicit and specific, is on the one hand not sumptuous and ornate and, on the other, not barren, impoverished, and grubby.

The trend toward the small community is an expression of a contemporary search for the heart. I see it as something that will pass because the heart, once awakened, will strike a spark that will find the limitations of an intimate group intolerable and stifling. I find a similar situation in the monastic search for the intimate group. To my mind it is a search for the heart and its awakening. Once this is attained the little circle will no longer be of value. A person needs space. It is already no small achievement to settle for a monastery and its restraining limits, while all agree that the solitary life is the ultimate achievement for the very intensity of its concern for the meeting of all the forces of heaven and hell, time and eternity, in the soul. Thus, the historic picture of the monastery church—large, ample, noble—is not merely evidence of a past form, but expressive of a truth that too many perhaps pass over lightly, neglecting at the same time to accept the possibility of the intimate group, should this be called for within the context of a large, even a very large, monastery.

Space is, after all, not merely a matter of physical distances. One sort of space a monk must have, and it can be expressed beautifully in the dimensions of a church, a cloister, a refectory, a chapter room. But one also needs inner space, privacy. Without this people soon become impoverished, an impoverishment regrettably common in our day, the fruit of an insolent violation of decency which is often blithely identified as love, with the supine tolerance of this arrogance demanded as evidence of reciprocal love. This kind of space—respect, reverence, dignity—is necessary to stay alive. Many monastic customs are a great help in this.

For example, it is not that I would question the possible good in an occasional monastic get-together, be it in the form of gathering around the TV for some special program, a buffet supper, some beer or wine now and then with chatter, a picnic, some sort of communal cook-out. Yet we must know what we are about. We ought not miss the message of the choral geography: the two facing choirs, as in the church, in chapter, the refectory. While something can be said, for example, for the suggested small tables for two or three as refectory furniture in order to express love in fraternity, the choral form has something to offer also, we face one another in an open, living dialogue in God, and yet we keep our distance.

Granted the need for intimacy and personal contact, must I have another's feet at my shins before we can be said to love one another? There is a certain diffidence to be maintained about getting too close. When my brothers become 'buddies', may it not be a question as to whether I am asking in the monastic family for those joys and exchanges of heart which truly are the privilege of wedded love? A certain solitude, an ability to stand alone, is necessarily a quality of the monastic desert, and I think any weakening of this area is a weakening indeed.

In the present human condition love needs protection, and one protection is distance. Friendship in some circles in the world means a sharing of wives. This is love carried beyond limits. In monastic circles you may speak of love freely and you may seek to act it out in this way and that, but unless it be characterized by a solitary aspect, it is bound to get confused. It is simply asking too much of fraternal love to expect it to be rewarding the way human wedded love is rewarding. The desert shared with others is still the desert. This is not to say that the monastic life is alien to friendship, and friendship of a deep and intimate kind. Rather, it is to say that life in community becomes impossible if the general tone is not one of pure love expressed in a respect for one another, a reverence that does not presume too much and violate the privilege of privacy on the score of fraternal love.

There is a certain chaste dignity in love that does not force itself upon you, a love that does not find dignity and respect frustrating, but rather an aid and a boon. When we get too close to one another it is not monastic life which becomes impossible, but life itself.

The message, then, of the choral arrangement is not to be taken too lightly or missed. Nor is it to be thought of as belonging to another era. We may learn much in the art of love from it. It has certainly escaped no one that much of current intimacy is phoney, and that the cocktail party, presumably the most friendly of causual gatherings, has long been recognized as an empty ritual made tolerable only by fermented spirits, and is indeed the perfect symbol of false closeness.

It is not that trends in the direction of the heart are to be condemned or suspected, but they should be recognized for what they are, they should be seen as means, not as ends, they should be kept in some sort of balanced relationship to the entire life. If life from the 'head side' is to be changed, cure does not lie in turning wholly to the heart and being overcome by it, but in a gradual and measured opening of the heart to make a whole person and a whole life. And this, admittedly, is a difficult thing to do.

The whole field of religion will surely be taken with more seriousness as people come more into contact with their hearts, not so much in the service aspects of religious life as in the speculative, contemplative, and notably in the monastic form. The advances will not be merely in the active apostolate, which will be taken over more and more by the laity, but in the life of prayer, contemplation, quite removed from the scene of action. Moreover, this whole enterprise will be entered into with far more enthusiasm, generosity, and understanding than is currently the case, precisely because people will know better what they are about and will have all the excitement that pioneers know in discovering a new land.

That is why I see a kind of longing for a dream world of the past as a betraying of the best interests of people and God, the church and the monastic life. This desire to live with a cozy group, in intimacy, this reduction of the liturgy to a minimal, primitive rite barren of beauty, this stripping of all poetic and romantic aspects from the life, is a flight from all that people love best, for in such a setting a poet could only die.

And a human being is a poet. In a house of no beauty, no song, no dance, no drama, no poetry, no mysticism, the person could only perish as in a prison with no gates. The fact that such smaller places are generally envisioned as encompassing some apostolate (the poor, the slums, the inner city) only seems to highlight a turning from masculine spiritual enterprise to maternal concern for the practical.

Man needs beauty, rite, splendor, ceremony, music, dance. It is part of his being. And it is precisely because man today has lost so much of this that women despise him. He is no longer a poet, a romantic. He is a bore, convenient for income. He has become busy, busy all day long, like mother's little helpers. He does not know how to make love, does not know how to sing, has no flair for rite, for ritual.

Thus we must be careful lest we do the worst thing possible to monks and gradually deprive them of a splendid liturgy because they are afraid of it. Rather, we must encourage them to become more human, to learn the use of leisure and to be wary of too much work. We should indeed do all that is required to sustain ourselves and provide for our guests and the poor. Then, content with plain living, learn what it is to be free and enter with glad hearts into the joys of song and dance, of rite and ritual, as becomes the sons of God. To learn the art of love, the finest art. Yet, to do this we must make use of all the traditional elements if we are to grow: discipline, fasting, abstinence, denial, rigor, silence, solitude, quiet reading—all essential and elemental. Without them the thing is impossible, for these are the tools of heroic endeavor. Yet these activities must flow from personal inner conviction and determination, rather than from rule and authority. And on the other hand, contact with the heart through work in service, in kindness, patience, and tolerance.

And since the eremitical life is the logical follow-up of the communal life, we can prepare to see a great flourishing of hermits, people committed to an entirely solitary life, engaged in the dialogue of love not through any fears or by way of flight, but by an ability to hold their ground alone by dint of the experience of love in the community. After all, the hermit life is simply a continuation of response to the original call to leave all and follow Christ. The first action involves one in an inner city of people who set out on a similar enterprise. Through the experience of love, the human city becomes the city of God, and the way is prepared for one to go further out into the desert, there in the wilderness to resolve the hidden ambiguities and conflicts in a bold and naked contact with pure love, frail and naked before God Almighty. Hermits are the glory of the monastery and the evidence that the place is real, the test of its authenticity.

Monks, then, in contact with the heart in nature, in animals, but particularly in work and in loving service to one another in community, learn the way of love. Marriage is the usual meeting place of man and woman, of the head and the heart. But the monk encounters woman in the bride of Christ, the church, his spouse. Yet the contact with her must be one in which the individual is not overwhelmed by her. There must indeed be genuine contact, a real meeting, but only that. For the fire of love will burn bright only when the meeting is right. Only then is the poet set free, the contemplative, the mystic. If one does not meet her, one grows cold, hard, brittle, bitter, dead. To be overcome by her is to become earthly, practical, horizontal, busy, fussy, motherly.

It is perhaps because modern man has been overcome by work, work that is so heavily maternal and earthy, that he has become more woman than man. He must come back to his own world and become man again. To do this, he needs—the monk does—a setting, a splendid liturgy. And a splendid liturgy in our tradition means one of austere and noble beauty, simple and pure, chaste. Not ornate. Not elaborate.

In the unbalanced situation in which one is not a whole person we may also have some of the aspects of difficulty with the 'institutional church'. When churchmen are 'manly' the results are soon manifest not only in authoritarianism and excessive, arbitrary control, but perhaps also in a lack of heart that makes religious cult cold, turns Christ's teaching into formal theology and moralism, kills the contemplative and mystic spirit. Further, it will enter with power and impact into the world of Christian service and render it as efficient charity and organized goodness. In such a setting Christ is indeed a God truly hidden. Against such a religion, a person in contact with the heart will be most at odds; real woman will languish. The greater the reliance on authority, the more frequent the call to obedience, the more certain we can be that we are dealing with people whose hearts are not alive. And in this day can there be a greater sin than to be dead in the heart, for where is the Spirit more active?

A cold and heartless liturgy gone formalistic has done a great disservice to Christ, as great as cold and heartless Christians—orthodoxy of faith and perfection of rubric notwithstanding. But the remedy for cold-heartedness in the church lies not in abandoning it, but in awakening the heart! So too the answer to hypocrisy in men who go through the motions of love with dead hearts lies not in getting rid of the liturgical action, or even in getting rid of the men, but in awakening the heart.

Surely this is done primarily within, where in one's own depths one enters into the truly inner city and confronts the real 'poor of the land', walks bravely into the slums of the heart's desolation. This is indeed the fruit of silence and solitude, fasting and prayer, and can be done only by use of one's total resources, powers called into being by prayer, expressed in song and acted out in loving dialogue with the poor and wretched in one's own household. For if the truest poverty lies within us and the courage we manifest in accepting it is a most manly courage, the expression of love lies scarely at much greater distance, for begun within, it finds its answering echo in the world at our fingertips, at our elbow. Here is love's greatest test and poverty's most demanding judgment. Failure here is total failure, for the monk nowhere gives more excellent testimony to the love of God than in the acceptance of one's own self and that of the community in the bright light of reality that the desert sheds.

Love on the merely horizontal plane will eventually peter out and vanish unless it is consistently confronted with its opposite in the vertical worship of God, notably in the liturgy. So too, the worship of God which departs from contact with the heart of mankind in its total misery will grow sterile, hard, even bitter. There must be both. If it takes a man and a woman to make a marriage, it also takes a head and a heart to make a human being, a person. The monk, if one is to live in eternity, must realize there is no temptation more insidious and more likely than the one which would encourage abandoning one for the other. One must take both and by total effort keep them at the point of fusion where the light of God's glory welds all things together in love.

The monk thus lives in the wilderness with others, keeping the heart warm by kind service in work, keeping the poet alive and awake by a noble and pure worship of God, maintaining the fire at its greatest intensity by a life touched with ascetic ardor. So gradually one comes to know what it is to be a human, and learns the greatest art, the art of love. And having come so far, a person may be said at least to have begun doing what shall be done for all eternity, in heaven, where there shall be neither male nor female and where we are not given in marriage, but shall be as the angels, whole, one pure flame of love.

Making Love in Liturgy ❧

ERHAPS SOME CARE ought to be taken that we do not give undue emphasis to the place of what might be called the 'fatherless generation' in our reshaping of the monastic life. This seems to be an outlook that is of considerable size which, while important and necessary, is of transitory character, and if taken for more than its worth, could lead us far afield.

There is no question that a strong reaction against the over-intellectual, over-pragmatic, over-authoritarian, over-logical trends of the past has long since set in and become a genuine force in our day. It will grow stronger and have immense results. The new stress of heart, of feeling, of emotion, of experience, is long overdue. It is being supplied by a generation that is 'fatherless' in the sense that it springs from a setting in which the father was actually or for all practical purposes absent, one in which the mother was strong and dominant. We live in a time of growing numbers of such men, who, although widely differing in makeup, are nonetheless characterized by a feminine rather than a masculine point of view.

Among a host of characteristics we may note a lack of aggression and ambition, a kind of passive receptivity, a lack of interest in achievement and endeavor, a want of organizational qualities, a lack of leadership ability. Positively, there may be great human warmth, genuine experience of pity, mercy, and compassion. There will be concern for the weak and the downtrodden, those in need. There will be a horror of violence, conflict, and hostility.

One can see this type of person—and the number grows daily in size and importance—a leaning toward the monastic life, especially in the contemplative variety. It responds to many people's needs and desires.

But I believe we must take care lest we be over-impressed by what must necessarily be a passing stage. While no one can deny the changing and changed character of today's man, it would seem to me important to recognize this change as one of reaction which will in turn be followed by a further reaction.

Man is not woman, nor is woman man. That society is perhaps the healthiest society in which each is something of the other, when man is not wholly head, but also heart; and woman is not only heart, but also head. The real person is not all male or all female, but predominantly one, with strong components of the other.

If past generations have been too one-sided, with men and women far too alientated from one another, the answer does not lie in complete reversal of roles. We are at the moment acting out this reversal, but it is impossible that it continue in one direction; if it does this will mean the total collapse of our culture. What is far more likely, and to be hoped for, is that man will come to terms with woman (the woman in him), and woman with man (the man in her). Marriage, obviously, is where this drama is usually acted out. In the spiritual and mystical life it is achieved in virginity and celibacy. But the end is the same: the attainment of the *person* in love.

The current handling of roles for man and woman is transitory: the wholly unreal and unnatural situation brings forth a fitting response of confusion and rejection which is apparent in marriage as well as in the consecrated virginal state. Thus, there is something unhuman and degrading about a woman strong in hard, aggressive qualities and weak in tender love for the child at the breast, just as there is something distressing about a man wholly unable to lead and inspire, who is content to wash dishes and mind the baby. This is no matter of simply accepting roles only in terms of what we are used to. Man, it will be noted, still plants the seed in the woman; the woman still bears in the womb and nurses at the breast.

The present lack of balance will not endure because it cannot. But we shall not return to the old ways either. Rather, what is called for is the new man and the new woman. In each case, one open to the other within. Society today is in need not merely of the organizer and leader, the aggressive and dynamic hero, but also of the poet, the mystic, the person

of art and culture. Society today needs the woman who not only con-
ceives and bears a child, but who also shares her gifts in the world of affairs, in politics, in the fields of peace, poverty, and justice. It is toward
this new kind of person that we are moving; the present turmoil and
confusion is the matrix.

We cannot return to the old forms of all male man and all female
woman. This is impossible. We must rather develop the whole person.
And that is why, in the monastic setting, we must take care that we do
not take the wrong road. The prospects for monastic life of the contemplative sort look excellent, but we must prepare the ground properly and
so orient the life that we attract to it those called by God.

If we bear in mind that the monk is one called to a life of wholeness
and integrity which embraces both head and heart, the male and female
if you will, then we will be right in our bearings. The life must be something of both. On the one hand, rule and order, discipline, regularity,
work, fasting, silence, organization. These are the typically masculine
areas. But there must also be service, submission, obedience, humility,
tenderness, concern, charity, kindness. These are typically feminine.
And these two must be blended into one in the person, the monk who is
indeed a man, but a man open to the heart. The surest indication that
this has been attained will come in the liturgy, for it is here that a person
is most truly human.

Basically, man is a lover, and it is in the art of love that he most perfectly expresses what he is. Part of the reason for modern woman's contempt for man is that he does not know how to love. The art of love is
expressed not merely in aggression, in achievement, in prowess, in work
and organization. This is love, to be sure, but only the beginning of love.
Love is more perfectly expressed in poetry, in music, in song, in dance,
in drama. In the field of religion and worship this is summed up in one
word: liturgy. One is never more human than when involved in the act
of love, the love of God. It is the most beautiful thing on earth.

But it is only when it is real, that is to say, when the action stems directly from the heart. No one can deny that much past liturgy has been
cold-hearted rite and perfunctory ritual. I look forward with eager longing to a day of flourishing monastic life rich in a liturgy of great nobility
and purity, lived by men of extraordinary love. I am sure it is coming.

Meanwhile, in helping to build this new life, we must take great care that we do not betray the best that we have by paying too much attention to this generation, a generation that must be understood rightly, a generation necessary in bringing forth the new, but not one to be taken at face value. Too many of the 'fatherless' generation do not love, nor do they know how to love. With the masculine side weak and undeveloped this is understandable. They are often open, receptive, passive, tender, but wanting in that prowess and enthusiasm which are so necessary for the act of love. Their reaction to liturgy is their reaction to any scene of love-making: retreat. They fear it. They fear to be nourished, to be mothered, to be warmed. They are content to look, to watch, to view—but passively and from a safe distance. And if you challenge them too strongly and too insistently with invitations to the dance, to song, to get involved, you may find your pains resented.

I would say that to take such reactions seriously would be a great blunder, for we would give away the only thing that will attract the new person. This is a transitional stage and we must understand that.

And we must take precautions lest we do the wrong thing for the right reason, for it will be strongly attested that the desire to 'be let alone', the desire for the simple, the plain, for a liturgical life reduced to the minimal level—that all this stems from a genuine contemplative spirit.

It will be maintained that this diffidence in the art of love is at root a contemplative orientation. Hardly anything could be more mistaken. The contemplative is nothing if not someone proficient and far advanced in the art of love. One who has been raised to such stages will, to be sure, find less and less need of external rite, gesture, word, and will engage in love primarily in his heart, anywhere, at any time. But to attain to such a level of love demands one who has achieved maturity in the spirit, a person in the fullest sense. Diffidence in liturgical prayer is no more sign of a contemplative spirit than diffidence in work.

One who fears love and the art of love can scarcely be called a man, let alone a person. This does not mean that the achievement of person and the art of love is tantamount to an enthusiastic embrace of the liturgical life. No. But it is close to it. For what is liturgy, but making love?

It is one thing to question the quality of liturgical action—the character, the modality, the appropriateness—but quite another to reject liturgy out-of-hand, endeavoring to reduce it to a few barren forms. That the liturgy has needed renewal, no one has questioned. The gradual reshaping and refashioning of it has been a great work of the Spirit of God. But we need to see clearly the role of the monastic life and the place of the liturgy in it in a day in which the orientation of the human personality is being seriously redirected. We need to prepare for the new humanity and to be ready for it. The transitional person, the fatherless one, must be seen to be just that, for in the coming age, the monk will truly be the son of his father and the son of his mother, will himself be a person of the head and of the heart, a great lover.

The monastery is a school for love, and the core of the monastery and its life of work and prayer is the holy liturgy. It is here that one learns the art of love and is prepared, should God so will, for the still more noble life of solitude in the hermit cell, where one engages directly in dialogue with the God of love. That is why the test of the monastery's authenticity will lie in its response to the call to solitude; the test of the monk's growth in love is response to the call of the liturgy.

The task, then, is not merely to provide a liturgy that contemporary 'fatherless' humanity will respond to, nor even to get one to respond to the liturgy, but to provide such a liturgy as is good for the whole person in the best tradition and patiently school the individual in it. This is no small task. It may even be that we are destined to spell the problem out at much greater length and see an almost complete devastation before the new man and the new liturgy arrive. I hope not. Certainly the duty we have to tradition and to handing on a patrimony ought to see us valiant in the endeavor to retain all that is good, loyal to the trust, and passing to those after us not merely what they like, but, in the best sense, what is good for them, good for them as human persons.

❧ Monks I Have Known

A Letter on the Death of
Thomas Merton ॐ

WE BURIED FATHER LOUIS [Thomas Merton] yesterday out back
of the monastery church on a slope under a cedar, in full view
of the wooded hills he loved. Odd, for it just struck me as I
type this that he should be buried there, where there is no wall to ob-
struct the view. The part of the cemetery enclosed by the wall right behind the church was filled some years back. Father Louis is out in the
open where you can see the beauty of the surrounding country. Fitting.

The funeral was at 3:30 in the afternoon and began on time. It was
pretty near dark when we got to putting him in the ground, and there
were just a few raindrops falling as we did so. It was damp and about
thirty degrees cold, I would guess.

The rite was joyous—no other word will do. There were about forty
concelebrants and the archbishop was there although he did not wish to
function. He said it was for us. There were quite a few guests in the
nave, invited ones, representatives of the worlds in which Father Louis
operated: writers, poets, artists, peace people, nuns, priests, publishers,
plain people.

He died far away in the midst of concern for the monastic life in the
east. His death was confused; I mean we are not really sure what he died
of: heart attack, accident with the electric fan? But we rest content with
the verdict that the death was accidental. There was some talk of an au-
topsy in the early confusion. Imagine trying to arrange something like
that on a phone to Bangkok. That slowed up his return. There were
frustrating delays, and he got here just in time for his funeral. The coffin
was not opened, so it turned out that I was right when I saw him leave
and said to myself, 'We will never see him again'.

Father John Eudes, our own medical doctor, looked at him in Louisville. Father Louis is the only one buried in a coffin in our cemetery that
I know of, which is like him! The coffin was one of those typical
monsters you would think were turned out in the shops of Metro-
Goldwyn-Mayer. The readings from the Book of Jonah in the Mass
were appropriate. There was the whale in front of us with Father Louis
inside.

Father Dan Walsh, who was the man's first link with Gethsemani,
preached a good homily and kept it sober and dignified. It all went well
and it was rich in significant things for us. There was a Mozart interlude
while the priests got out of their vestments for the burying and it sat well
on the heart.

I do not know how to summarize the man; the thought is not even
decent. Except to say that he was a contradiction. He lived at the center
of the cross where the two arms meet. Maybe, you could say, at the
heart of life. My guess is that at no other place is contradiction reconciled.

He was a problem to many here and elsewhere. I know the reason for
the problem: I mean the terrifying tensions the man endured with a kind
of courage that only the power of God made possible. I kept feeling
when close to him that God is near. And to be near God is to be near
something at once wonderful and terrible. Like fire. It burns. People
were forever trying to get out of the spot he made for them (by simply
being what he was) by putting him into some category or other and then
making him stay there. About as good as bottling fog! They would
decide that he is a 'monk' and this is what a monk should do. Then they
would expect him to do it. And he wouldn't. Couldn't.

When he became a hermit they would decide what a hermit is and
then they would see if he was being a good hermit. And he would not
be! The only way I could live with the man was to love him whole, as
he was, with all his contradictions, and I think this is the only way to
understand him. That is the way he loved me.

He was as merry a man as I have known, yet he had depths of sadness
it were best not to mention. He loved the monastic life, yet lived it in a
style all his own. He had a real love for the solitary life, and yet no one
around here has his kind of love for people, for the world God made.

He was above everything trivial and petty, and yet he kept up with everything and knew all that was going on. He could be as tough as any one, yet was as gentle and tender as a child with a bird. He could be flippant and airy, but he could also freeze you with his intensity and ardor. He had the jaunty walk of a man in his twenties, but I do not know many with the sense of compassion that he had. He loved the monastery, yet was critical of its foibles and foolishness. He would argue and plead with his abbot the way a shrewd lawyer would argue for a lost cause, yet he was obedient to the core of his being. His obedience was tested time and time again and found pure.

I cannot go on. You do not get this kind of person from the hands of God very often. He is a living witness for God, for Gethsemani, for the monastic life, for the church, for the world. Praised be God in his saints forever and ever. Amen.

FATHER JOHN THE BAPTIST'S FIFTIETH ANNIVERSARY OF ORDINATION ⅋

A sermon preached in July, 1968

A PRIVATE THEORY of my own by which I sustain my courage in a troubled time is that all of my contemporaries will be saved. That is to say, everyone who has lived on the earth during the same time I have will attain the kingdom. This may indeed be somewhat bold, but I root it in the Gospel and in Christ's saying that we can have whatever we ask for. It is as simple as that: I am asking for the salvation of everyone. It is of course obvious that I have a share in the work involved, a share which may indeed be modest in any sense, but none the less essential, and no matter how difficult it may be. It is this dimension of reality that gives a kind of tension to life: the endeavor always to be and to do what I ought, for one never knows what is involved in what one is asked to bear, to do, to suffer. To the end of life, then, one always has the sense of obligation to an unknown individual.

But then something like today's feast comes along and sets everything right, for the work accomplished by Jesus is also shared by an unknown number of souls. Here is one who for fifty years has been offering the sweet sacrifice on the altar of God for others. Think of what that means! I mean in faith. As people of flesh and blood, we do of course set great store on such things as the language of the Mass, the style of vesture, the direction we face, and whether we offer it alone or with others. These are trivial aspects. It is the happening that is of consequence, I mean the oblation of Jesus Christ, man and God, to the Father, carried on through time. What a great joy on earth! What a source of blessing!

Yes, the works of people are needed; it is good to build and create. It is good to eat and drink, to marry and give in marriage. It is good to play as it is to work, to teach and preach and organize. This horizontal dimension is very much the dimension of our day. But there is also another direction to the tree of life. It must also go up, up to God, to the Father. It is this dimension which must also be present if we are to have the cross of Christ. We are warned of this today in the Gospel when Christ upbraided the Pharisees who neglected one aspect and stressed the other. Love of neighbor, yes. But sacrifice to God, also.

This is to be a priest: not to preach, not to shrive, not to teach, not to lead, not even to guide and console, but first and foremost to offer the sacrifice. This presence of the hidden God on earth is our greatest treasure, our finest blessing. A mysterious reality that cannot be measured, cannot be fathomed, escapes all our endeavors to categorize and rationalize. What a glorious grace for Gethsemani to have this priest among us who for fifty years has stood at the altar. This is the fundament that holds everything together, this is the rock upon which our faith is founded, this is the salvation of mankind.

Let our joy be great this day and our faith deepened. If we join Father John and in the priesthood we all share extend our hands over the bread of what we are, the wine of what we have, and the water of what we do, we become one with the redeeming Lord who would not have a single soul lost. Neither would you. Neither would I. Let us go then to the altar with the joy of youth.

OUR LAST CHRISTMAS
WITH DOM JAMES* ॐ

I
N THESE LONGEST DARK NIGHTS of the year it is good to have a moon
in the sky. I am not sure why we have a moon, but it sure is nice to
see it shining through the windows of the church during Compline.
It is nice to step outside after Matins for a moment of mystery before
coffee, to linger in the moon shadows and wonder why God is the way
he is. I could ask my head, 'why is the moon', but the head's answer
would not touch my heart, and it is my heart which is asking. But my
own heart would tell me, if I would listen a bit. It would tell me that the
moon is to make us wonder about the other side of things. For who can
look at the moon whose face has been turned toward us since the night
it first rode through the sky and not wonder what is on the other side of
the moon? We do not know. But we are learning. And still it poises
there as an eternal testimony to the old word: there are two sides to
everything, the side you see and the other one.

This is our last Christmas together. This is the last time we will gather
in this chapter room on a Christmas Eve and prepare for the feast of the
Lord's nativity, the last time we as monks will gather with our abbot in
a spirit of love and joy in entering into the greatest of Christian mysteries. We must therefore make the most of this feast, since it is the last
time.

But of course that is only partly true, for besides being the last time it
is also the first time. We have never celebrated this Christmas. We have

*Dom James Fox, who was soon to retire as Abbot of Gethsemani to take up the life of
a hermit.

82

never gathered on this particular day in this particular place with these particular people under these particular circumstances. This event, after all, is unique. It is a first.

But it is also a last. It will never come back; never be repeated, something that can be but once and, having been, will always be that, nothing more, nothing less. In a sense this is true of all that happens on the earth. Everything is but once, a kind of simultaneous first and last. Every new day is that, every night. Every bird song. Every drop of rain.

It is this aspect of alpha and omega that we must take pains to love if we would grasp the wholeness of life. Things are not always what they seem, they are a great deal more. If you see only the alpha side you see but one side. If you see only the one aspect of first, you neglect the aspect of last.

The joy of this event today is that it is the first time; its sadness is that it is the last. It is perhaps the constant confrontation of the passing and the permanent that is our first taste of eternity. For eternity is the permanent first and last, eternity is the never-ending newness and oldness of all things in perfect combination. Eternity is the constant love song of what God is and what is not God, a dialogue rooted in the uniqueness of God and the uniqueness of everything created in his likeness.

For you are like God not only because you are but also because like God there is only one of you and there can be no other. You are just like God in that you are and yet you are not like God at all, for he always was and always will be. Yet, if you do not exist, God does not either, for God's existence has been given another dimension because you are and because you give witness to the existence of God. Yet God is no greater for it.

If we play with these truths, the interaction of contradictions, we perhaps in some way come to mark the dimensions of the mystery we are concerned with in these holy days: the coming to earth of him who is everywhere, the birth of him whose life has no beginning, the incarnation of him who is pure spirit. The Almighty is now an infant, the Infinite Wisdom is a suckling child at the breast, the Creator of all things the object of musing by quiet cattle munching their cud and watching with gentle eyes.

The Christian, then, far from avoiding the anguish of trying to reconcile what cannot be reconciled, knows that in this very tension, in this very meeting of opposing forces, the truth is born.

Life is not one-sided. It is ambivalent. There is a polarity which demands that two must meet in a dialogue of love. God is one and three. Christ is God and humanity. Mary is virgin and mother. Birth in Christ is a kind of dying. Death in Christ is the way to life. In the midst of suffering one can have true joy; in the midst of conflict one can know true peace. The road to Calvary is a glory road. The setting sun is the only way to have a rising one. The only way to get anything is to give everything away.

There is a kind of elemental dialogue that seems to be deep in the nature of all reality. It is a dialogue which implies not merely a meeting, but a meeting in which the truth emerges not from one dominating the other but from each meeting the other in love and communing, avoiding mere submergence and disappearance into the other, or forcing the partner to disappear into one's own being. There is a sense in which we must hold our ground and insist on the genuineness of what we are, but it is an insistence that takes into account the other's right also to be what he is. It is in the meeting that the whole truth is born.

Uniformity, then, is not characteristic of the work of God. It is only a human being who cares to turn out a million cans of tomato soup and takes pride in the undoubted truth that one tastes exactly like another. God, on the contrary, delights in variety. He does not delight in uniformity and repetition. So simple a thing as an oak leaf must be unique and singular, different from every other oak leaf. God takes glorious delight in the individual, the specific.

People are fearful of the different. They tend to like people like themselves, settle for friends of their own kind, their own culture, their own race and background, their own field of labor. We enjoy friends who think as we do, whose enemies are our enemies, whose God is our God. We fear the stranger, the unknown, the unexperienced. Who does not relish the comfort of an old and familiar shoe, the routine we are used to, the rite we are familiar with? Yet, even if we acknowledge all this, we know too that it is not the whole story.

People also love the strange place and the strange people. They love to investigate and to explore. They invent, create anew. They are curious and inquisitive, wonder about the other side of the moon. They enjoy talking to people from far away places. For all their reaction against change there is a side to people that loves change. If they love order and regularity, it is just as true to say that they have a hankering sometimes for confusion and chaos. People will put up a building and not long afterwards tear it down, monks included.

It is undoubtedly in our own life that we find the greatest need to reconcile differences through an act of love. One of the hazards in coming apart into a desert place is that there we more readily see things as they are. Lacking the pleasant distractions and diversions of the good life, we have more attention available for the things that matter. This is not always easy to bear, but it is one of the elements for building a life of deep love. For all that, it would be a childish delusion to pretend that the person of the street and the person of the everyday world do not taste the mystery of God's strange ways. Indeed, too often it seems that one tastes him with an intensity that makes one shudder and wince. If, then, we who have responded to an invitation to follow the Lord into the wilderness should there discover that the dimensions of God's activity include much that is unfathomable, we ought to be glad, having, as it were, come to know him better and therefore to love him more.

It is not merely the disastrous aspects of our own persons that threaten us and fill us with confusion, but the vision of the same forces in others. The whole of life seems to add up to a bundle of contradictions. This seems particularly true today when a strange Providence has decreed for our own time an element of chaos and confusion that at times seems to overwhelm us. And we who perhaps thought of religion as a safe harbor, a quiet haven, discover that far from that it seems rather to be at the very eye of the hurricane that sweeps around the world.

When we begin to get a grasp of these aspects of reality—and God knows that no one escapes them—we ought to take heart. We are at least alive. That is a great deal. Only the dead and demented could escape the tensions of our day.

But having discovered them, then what? Why, you do what everyone else does. You keep on dancing. You keep on singing. The game goes on. You put a smile on your face and you just keep right on going. You do your work and you say your prayers and you read your book and

life goes on. You be as kind to others as you can because they are in the
same world you are in and may be finding it more bewildering than you
do.

Night is a part of day, and tears a part of laughter. Suffering is a kind
of joy, and misery a touch of the divine. We have two feet to keep us
upright in a staggering world, two ears to listen carefully to both sides of
everything, two eyes to get a good look from every point of view, two
arms to accept what comes, two shoulders to bear bravely the burdens
of life, one mouth to praise God and not curse.

It is Christ who pulls everything together and makes sense of all
things. Not by denying what is, but by reconciling all things in love.
And when we read the Gospels, we are amazed to discover how many
times he expressed in contradiction the truth that he is. Indeed, his
whole life seems a bringing together of heaven and earth, humanity and
God, time and eternity, suffering and glory.

Christmas ought to mean a wondering on these things and a quiet
dwelling with them in our hearts. They are not things we can understand and therefore there is little point in thinking about them or in trying to figure them out. You dwell with them, you ponder them, you
turn them over and over in your heart.

The upshot of that can only be a great strength and a great peace.
There is strength because the acceptance of reality always reduces our
fears of it. Nothing is hard once you admit it. Peace comes in the Lord
because we discover that in the midst of reality sits the humble Saviour.
There in the bombed out ruins of our own particular desolation, there
in the midst of the chaos and the confusion of our times stands the humble Christify, serene and calm. His message is one of peace. It sounds
almost out of place. Irreverent. Yet, I see him and I hear him say it.

So, you look at the Child in the crib, you look at his Mother, you
look at the man named Joseph, you look at the surrounding scene. And
then you try to remember what is coming in thirty years or so. At that
point you stop your fussing and fuming. You had a better birth than he
had. You will have a better death. It is becoming then, is it not, for you
and for me to taste in between a bit of the human condition? And if we
do, what greater joy can there be?

That is why you cannot blame someone who would like to go apart and be alone not to nurse wounds, not to count victories, but rather quietly to take all the mysterious fabric of his life and there lay it all out and trace the hand of love that somehow ordered all things, the good and the bad, the crooked and the straight, the bitter and the sweet, the whole of it . . . and then to take the whole thing and throw it over one as a garment woven in love.

Have a good Christmas, reverend Father; have a good Christmas, my brothers. This is the last time. And the first.

May the rising sun brighten all your days.

May the moon soften the darkness of your nights. Amen.

SOLITUDE

THE DINNER PARTY 🦢

I AM WRITING THIS in Thomas Merton's hermitage. It is a Wednesday morning in January. The sun is shining brightly; there is snow on the ground and it is about twenty-two degrees outside. There is a fire in the fireplace to my right and outside on the porch birds are eating the bread crumbs that I scattered there. I can look down the valley and over beyond the ridge three or four miles away the other side of New Hope. There is a light blue haze about and it is every bit a beautiful morning, handsome enough to make any number of fine photos for a lovely color calendar scene to hang on your wall. It is warm and pleasant here in the sunshine by the big window. I have the big bass guitar that someone brought along from Mexico and left in the guest house for us. I have my silver flute. I strum the one now and then or toot the other. It is harmless.

Father Louis, as we used to call Merton, talked sometimes of Camus, but I never read anything of his. He did a study of *The Plague* for a reading program of the Seabury Press, and I read that yesterday. It was very good, but *The Plague* was gone from the library so I must wait. I did get *The Fall* and other stories and I read them last night by the fire and this morning. I come up here after supper and stay until dinner time, so I have a few days to myself.

I have been living with Camus these past few days and am haunted by the mystery of sin. When I was in the library I saw a few photos of the Viet Nam war and some items in *The Critic* of priests in vestments being taken by the police. I regret that I do not keep up with the news and with events. I should and I encourage the juniors to do so, but I do not find the time and you cannot do everything. But the war and the chaos of our own time does not escape me.

91

I am much concerned with the mystery of evil. I believe in the evil spirit. I say the Mass of the Angels every time I have Mass by myself, for I believe in angels too. They are as much a part of my world as birds and butterflies, trees and lakes. So are the evil ones who move about on our landscape, in our hearts and in our country.

A monk must reckon with the powers of darkness. You cannot just pretend that they are not there. The reason I have such a profound faith in angels and their good influences in our behalf is that I have a far more profound belief in the evil spirits. It is because of the power of Satan in our world that I have to believe in angels. To live without angels is to live without poetry, without beauty. My word, I should believe in electricity and not in angels? I should know of cancer silently eating the heart out of my neighbor and not believe in the evil one?

If I had no other reason, there is my own heart where there are shadows enough and dark times and dark influences that frighten me and are answered only by trust in God and his grace, his holy mother and all our friends, the saints of heaven, the angels.

As I sit here I am aware that Father Louis is around. I do not see him, I do not hear him. There are no voices, no visions, so subtle tricks. But he is here all the same. When he went to Bangkok he took along a dozen or so relics of saints he loved: hermits and monks and martyrs and confessors and virgins. He had a simple sort of faith. The saints were close to him. The angels. But they are close to all of us. Always. We have only to realize it. When we do that we are best able to cope with the powers of evil.

Sin is real. It is a mighty power and an awful influence. It is hideous and monstrous and diabolical. It is to bomb innocent people and set fire to houses and kill children. It is to rob and steal and strike down. It is to give full vent to hatred and anger. It is to connive and plot and destroy. Sin burns lovely paintings and blows up libraries. I do not understand sin, but I believe in it. I fear it. I fear its influence in me, through me, on me.

We cannot be blind to evil. I doubt if we can understand it, but we must never grow immune to it. There is the constant temptation to do so because it is so very hard to comprehend. It would be a help to us if we could write it off. That is why we must return again and again to our own hearts. Sin is not something others do. It is a capacity we all have. It has strong roots within us, ready at any time to bloom and to flourish. It is silly and dreadful to click your tongue at sin in others. Go look in a mirror when you feel like getting righteously indignant at sin.

I go to my hermitage each morning from after Terce until Sext.* It is a real break and I enjoy it. I work then in the afternoon in the shoe house. In the hut I pray or read or muse or wonder or reflect or ponder or what have you.

However, there are times when it is all I can do to go out there. There is some strange power that frightens me and makes me want to beg off, for I fear it. I always go and in the end I find that going out to meet it drives it away.

I link that in some way with evil. There is something strange here. I mean there is no doubt in my mind that there is evil within us, and yet we must face it, meet it, reckon with it, in Christ. And when we do that, all will be well. But woe to us if we hide it or cover it up or smooth it over or pretend it is not there! It will out! It will out indeed, for if it will not be recognized in one way it will be in another.

These are the things a monk must wrestle with. There are no doubt demons in the desert. To deny this is foolhardy in the extreme. But, on the other hand, we are not to be frightened by them. We have Christ and the saints and the holy angels.

This dimension of sin is a dimension of reality that we must cope with. It is folly in the extreme to try to make of the monastic life some mild, tame form of religion in which we live in a kind of somnolent peace with nothing but the sound of the wind blowing or the crickets chirping or our own snoring to disturb us. There is a constant temptation to make our life nice. We do not want to be wealthy or lazy or without responsibility or labor, but we sure would like to have it nice. In the madness of the times that seems not too wild a request. We may, however, be heading for delusion and disaster if we try to build a monastic life that ignores the satanic touch. There is no doubt whatever, absolutely no doubt, that angels hover over this house. But there is no doubt either, no doubt whatever, that the evil spirits are not far away.

*i.e. mid-morning until noon.

I am trying hard to say that evil is part of the human scene.

Recently one of our brothers decided that his vocation was no longer with us. We have had a number of departures, as most monasteries have had, and I think we have been able to accept this. The times are troubled and that means they are times of judgment. In times of judgment it is sometimes given to a person to see that he is not where he belongs. In a more peaceful era he might have managed well enough, but there is a tension to our day that clarifies things and brings things into focus. This must not distress us. It is a good thing, but it is not always pleasant.

This does not mean that every departure is a good one, but at least one does feel that people are more willing in our day to see that a change of state is not out of the question. In any case Brother was a good soul and in the abbey many years, twenty or so. He was rather childlike in many ways and really quite tender and sensitive. He told a neighboring couple that he knew that he was leaving and going back home. The woman said to him, 'Brother, I want to tell you something. You are a very good soul and very open and generous. I just want to warn you: take care. Not everyone in the world is good. There are evil people and they will be quick to take advantage of you.' The Brother blanched a bit, but he got the message. And indeed he needed it. He received it from one capable of giving it. Had a monk told him he would not have been impressed.

The lesson was a good one, and true. There are evil people around. We forget that, living in a monastery. We get, as it were, extremely naïve. Generally, only the abbot and the cellarer keep their feet on the ground, for they have enough contact with the world of human affairs to keep things balanced. This does not mean that I advocate general overall contact in order to keep balanced; there are other ways of doing it. But the point remains: there are few totally evil people and few totally good. There is good and bad in all.

We know that this is true also of ourselves. We can let ourselves be caught off guard because there is a quality of genuine goodness in our lives. A group of people living together for many years come to smooth off the rough edges, adjust to one another, learn patience and a certain kindness and tolerance. They practice service and generosity and a whole host of monastic virtues.

This is not just a matter of environment, yet who would deny that environment has a lot to do with it? There would perhaps be facets of my character and yours which would surprise both you and me were we to live in a concentration camp for two or three years.

I experience myself as almost another person when in community and when alone in the woods. No doubt we are one thing in the monastery and another out of it. That is not bad, but it suggests that there are aspects that can be quieted or muted or coaxed to lie dormant. The same can be said of evil. It is within us. It may be buried, silent, stilled. But do not be deceived. The potency is there, the capacity. Given the occasion, we do not know what we are capable of in terms of good or evil.

An awareness of this dimension should not be a crippling experience, but a deepening one, an enriching one. Our capacity for sin is a human dimension. It is a potency all people share. In some the potency is actualized more than in others, that is all.

Within our lifetime the evil in people has been more manifest than at perhaps any other time in history. This is a dark age in the very truest sense of the word, advances of the most magnificent kind notwithstanding. If people have shown themselves almost infinite in their capacity for achievement, their capacity for evil has also kept pace and done very well. People have changed very little. They have simply become more effective.

Since we are human, this capacity for both good and evil is in us also. We have committed ourselves to the good life, to the pursuit of noble ideals and the following of a road of peace with everyone and with the worship of God in truth. Notwithstanding, we can never forget who we are and what we are. We must keep the channels of communication open to our own hearts. It is the heart that hides all the secrets. I believe the ancient monastic term for this was compunction.

My hermitage in the woods is the old pump house by Dom Frederic's lake. The little house is at the bottom of the cement dam which holds back the water in a deep gorge and forms a relatively large lake. The pump house has the valves and at one time had the pumps to help the water over to the monastery and up into the water tower. So I took over the little house, about twelve by eight feet and ideal. Back of me, then, and above is the lake, large and beautiful and surrounded by woods.

In front of me is a little pool where some run-off water gathers and where cows used to drink years ago. It is small, very deep and full of rotten matter. I call it 'compunction pool', just as the other is the 'joyous lake'. It is there in front of me to look at. It is very lovely and is shaded over in summer with trees and vines. But it is black and deep and full of mystery.

I have stripped and plunged into it a few times and come out covered with a black dye from the boggy matter. Then I ran up to the joyous lake and washed it away. I think we need to plunge into our own depths like that now and again. We need this contact with darkness. It is not evil, for we can have no truck with evil. Perhaps it could be called a potency for evil, an available source of it. It is not like allowing ourselves to get a little angry so we can enjoy keeping our anger in control. Nor like getting a little drunk to prove we can maintain sobriety. That would be like going without Mass and Communion to prove we can do it. There is something sick in that attitude.

No, it is rather a very healthy thing. It is like having children of whom you are rightly proud. You have complete confidence in them, and yet you see in them plainly enough a capacity for evil. You do well to point it out, but in a way that does not crush or dishearten. This is a sort of healthy realism that is neither morbid nor naïve. It is simply wise and mature.

It is adolescent to surrender to evil powers within you. To live without an awareness of evil is to live in a child's fairy wonderland. Seeing adults blindly giving in to their appetites for food or drink or flesh or possessions is disgusting. To witness that mass madness in which all the latent hatreds within a person are set free in violence is to be filled with horror. Our age is simply proving that the worst thing to do is to drive evil underground and hide it from view and pretend that it does not exist. The whole body becomes sick and covered with the long-hidden leprosy.

We are quite as capable as the next person of this sort of thing. There is not one of us who has any real grasp of what we are able to do once properly prepared, once the passions have been aroused. Perfectly good people in a mob become monsters. It is like the keeper of the concentration camp who had flowerbeds at the entrance to the camp and a grand piano in his room because he had a taste for fine music. The ordinary person has a capacity for evil that one is not aware of under normal circumstances.

The monk must experience and become aware of this, or he will live only on the edge of life, on the surface, merely skimming along. No one is worse off than the skimmer who thinks he has all the answers, is full of confidence. The ice, alas, is so very thin and brittle, and the lake so deep and the water so cold.

There is something refreshingly sound about a person who knows what he or she is. There is nothing degrading about recognizing the capacity for evil in oneself. What is degrading about being in need of redemption? It is a fact, and to know that we need it is an asset, not a handicap. Whose love for the Redeemer is more fragile than one who has no grasp of one's own misery?

The great upheaval of our time is basically a monastic experience. The whole world is being exposed to the vision of humanity as it is. All the inner hatreds and corrupt rottenness is being brought out into the open and put on the screen for all to see. No one is spared. It is a world of wide exposure. You simply cannot live today in any kind of expectancy that you are to get through life without living. It is impossible to live in these times without having some grasp of the human condition. To avoid this vision would be pure betrayal of a monk's vocation.

The very blazing light of God is shining on us and revealing us for what we are. This revelation is wholesome and good. It will not ruin the Church, but it will purify it. It can be said in truth, the heat is on. So is the light. For the monk, however, this should be the natural course of events. He should aim to live within the light of the truth.

It is a lot simpler to believe in angels when you are aware of how great is our need for them. People who make a tea party of the religious life see no need for belief in the devil, the evil one, or the evil in a person's heart. While they drink their tea the fires of hell are raging all over the world. We flutter on the edge of doom and fuss because the soup is cold.

Having met the evil of our day in my own heart, in the hearts of others, and in the world, I go out and stand under the sky. I listen to the chirping of the birds as I throw some crumbs to them. The sun is bright on the snow. The pines are rich against the cold sky and I wonder why it is the way it is. The sun warms my skin as it warms the cold earth and all the things that sleep in it until spring, and I try to fathom the strange mystery of evil. I do not have an answer. I only know that one had better reckon with it, otherwise the dinner party will turn into a nightmare and we will not know why.

The Dalai Lama and Dom Vital ॐ

I RECENTLY READ a fascinating book by Heinrich Harrer called *Seven Years In Tibet*. We had read in the refectory the memoirs of the Dalai Lama, whom Father Louis had visited and about whom most of us knew practically nothing. This book, too, was very interesting, particularly for a monk, and it was because of it that I was led to pick up the one by Harrer.

The man was German. As a youth he was full of love of exploit and prowess and had determined to excel in sports. As it turned out he was very good in many, but above all in mountain climbing. As a child he had known the Alps. Eventually he heard that a team would go to the Himalayas to climb some unmastered peak there, and he was determined to get a place on it. Since he was unknown he climed a 6,700 cliff in the Alps and by this feat was recognized as having exceptional abilities. As a result, he was invited to join the team going to the Himalayas.

While the group was in India on the way back from a scouting trip World War II broke out. As German citizens in a British area the men were interned. Since conditions seemed to worsen as time went on Harrer made up his mind to escape and go to Tibet. He failed twice, but the third time he succeeded.

The story of the long trek by foot across the Himalayas into Tibet, a journey of some thousand miles, makes reading that is exciting and hardly believable. He was a foreigner in a forbidden land, without means and resources, unprotected by his own home country, alone except for a companion in the same condition.

The two men wanted to reach the inner hidden city of Lhasa and only after the most severe effort did they reach it. It took them two years.

They were received at first with some misgivings, then with astonishment and eventually with warmth and enthusiasm. They found a place in Tibetan life and won admiration for their services in engineering and landscape gardening. Eventually Harrer became a private tutor to the Dalai Lama, then a boy of fourteen or fifteen.

Harrer and his companion found life in Lhasa fascinating in the extreme, far removed from anything they had known in Europe. The people were a marvelous combination of earthiness and mysticism. They loved ritual, rite, ceremony, and display. The whole life was woven around their love for Buddhism and their interest in the spiritual dimension, full of ancient customs and practices. The country had literally thousands of monks and there were monasteries everywhere. Though the economy was simple, the people were well fed and, for all its simplicity, their life was a good one by any standards.

The people had delved deeply into the mysteries of the unconscious and had many strange techniques for manifesting the human heart, using them in the very running of civil and domestic affairs.

One can only feel, as Harrer felt, that he had discovered hidden away in the deep mountains of Asia a secret city where there was joy and serenity, where people were good to one another, where peace was paramount. They were a people without aggressive designs, content to live on their own mountains, wholly lacking in any desire to do other than live out their own lives in tranquility. They knew nothing of modern warfare and of the violence that has swept with such devastation over the whole of Europe twice in our century, continues in Asia, and plagues even our own land yet.

After five years in this paradise it became evident that all was not well. The Chinese Communists had plans of taking over Tibet and eventually did so, simply annexing the helpless country. The Dalai Lama fled to India. So did Harrer and his companion. The Tibet that used to be is no more. There are no more monks there. All seems finished.

I lived with these things for a long time and thought much about them. I could not help making the obvious connection between the exploit Harrer was engaged in and the monastic calling. Certainly the journey into the hidden city is as good a picture as we need. All of us have entered on such a journey, to search for such an inner city. That it should involve a person in a number of preliminary difficulties and hazards to overcome and manage seems appropriate. The long hard journey is in fact a most fitting description of the monk's search for inner truth, for wholeness and integrity. While there is a sense in which the whole of the Tibetan people might be thought of as some large monastery, symbolized by the huge complex at Lhasa, it can just as well represent the monk's inner quest for life in depth in which he attains a kind of hidden city where dwells the divine. Certainly the joy and peace that Harrer knew in inner Tibet can only be some semblance of the serenity of the monk in his awareness that he has come into contact with some profound center of being which at once makes him wholly human.

There is no question in my mind that many of these people attained a spirituality of a high order and that they had a grasp of the contemplative aspects of the spiritual life far deeper than is common in the west. They were people of peace and of great love for nature. They would kill no living thing. There was dirt and disease, no doubt, and much childish superstition, and there was human failing for all to see. Still, the overall picture remains. One has the feeling that this was closer to what life is supposed to be than anything we have. At least Harrer, who came from one of the leading countries of Europe, was not so sure that we are as successful in the business of living as they.

So he attained this paradise, this cloister garden hidden in the mountains amid the snow and wind, and had great dreams of helping these people in matters of health, hygiene, and water supplies. He certainly brought them nothing in terms of the spiritual life though he was himself a man of integrity and great courage. It is clear as you read that the Tibetans respected him and it is to be noted that they permitted him direct contact with the Dalai Lama, something their own people did not have.

Then all this was destroyed.

Why?

Why was this permitted? These people had been in these mountains for uncounted centuries and had built up a life pattern with profound mystical overtones, doing no harm to anyone. They were unprotected and helpless.

There is no question that they were too remote from the world of people. The Dalai Lama said as much and would have opened up his land and his people to the world had the opportunity been given him. But the oppressors came first.

What happened in Tibet is almost standard in monastic experience. I do not mean merely that monasteries have often been pillaged, confiscated, secularized, and destroyed. Europe is covered with this sort of ruin. But again, is not this some working out of an inner experience?

Have you noticed that for many monks, the monastic life is taken away from them? There are many who leave the monastery, and I would suggest to you that there is a strange providence and a profound mystery at work here. In some who leave there may be at work some particular calling to an abandonment of all, a setting out on another journey every bit as much an exploit in love as the first.

It is my suspicion that after he has spent a good deal of time in seeking the monastic life and made profound growth in it, this is sometimes taken away from the monk. To put it in more pedestrian terms, you grow out of it. I believe there is a more perceptive attitude to this phenomenon today, and some poeple see in the solitary life some aspect of it. The solitary who finally leaves the cenobium in order to follow the road alone is in some way acting out what is going on within him, what is taking place within his own heart.

Every monk is going to experience this in some form or other if his monastic life is deep. It will be taken away from him. An enemy will come and deprive him of it. The significance or value or meaning that it once had for him will somehow disappear and there will be nothing left.

I would be so bold as to say that many who leave monasteries are quite mistaken in their understanding of what is happening. I believe that there are cases where one should leave, and sometimes the solitary life is a genuine aspect of the monastic experience. But many who make these choices are not truly aware of what has taken place within them and settle for inappropriate answers.

The infirmary is the place for you if you are sick. It may be that things have come to such a pass that leaving the life and the Order is the only thing to do. There will be those for whom the solitary life is a call from God. But I should serve you warning that these questions will come your way, too. Slowly and strangely something will come over you and you will be frightened by it. You may think that you are losing your faith or that you have lost your vocation. In the ensuing panic that may overwhelm you, you may make a very foolish step.

I would go further and say that this is a necessary and wholly healthy development in our spiritual life and one we must learn to recognize and appreciate. It is an invitation by divine grace to move further in and deeper down. It is a call to further abandonment and deeper commitment. It is an expression of love that is expected in someone who has given everything he had to Jesus Christ. This is the Lord coming to take what you have given.

If God sends you suffering and sickness the road is clear enough. If he sends you a calling to solitude, then get it confirmed by God's agents, the Church, before you act on it. You will not be the first fool or the last if you follow only your own counsel, least of all in this. But, if you are tempted to interpret all this as a sign that your vocation is no longer here, take great care. You may be spurning grace and not realizing it. I would not pass any judgment on anyone. God takes care of all and you do not have to be in a cloister to save your soul. However, take great ✓✓ care that you do not abuse grace and refuse a calling from the Lord.

Far too many today think that because the life has no meaning for them any more this is somehow a sign that they should leave [where they are]. It is, on the contrary, just the opposite. It is an invitation to probe more deeply into the life. It may be a call to purification and immolation, a call to love on far more intimate terms. This is to be asked to give up everything and follow the Lord, to plunge into the darkness in faith. This is to be asked to walk the lonely road and ascend to the hill with the Lord. Or, if you like, it is to die with him and to descend with him into the depths of hell.

To be sure, there are monks who have left who should have done just that, and perhaps a lot sooner. I am not simply recommending perseverance as the answer to all monastic problems. Nor am I saying that life in solitude is for every monk who grows into the monastic life. It is only a variant of the life he must live because that is the way God made him and the way God acts in him. Every monk, however, can expect a call to inner solitude in one form or another. When this day comes, let the monk stretch out his arms wide and say, 'Yes, Lord'. Then he may well be stripped of everything he loves.

I cannot tell you exactly how this happens; it has to be experienced. It is not easy. It is not that life becomes meaningless or a monstrous bore. No, it is far more subtle, far more lovely, far more interior. It is perhaps best described as a purification and a chastening in which one's attitudes change and a spirit of freedom results. In a sense life becomes easier, simpler, less annoying and provoking. One gets far less excited about things that happen. It is an ability to dance well and not take oneself too seriously.

While you dance you sense that the whole situation has changed. It is not only that you feel yourself disappearing, but your partner disappears, the people in the ballroom disappear, the roof goes off the place, and the whole thing opens up to infinite dimensions so that you feel as if you are dancing in heaven itself. Yet you dance still. In other words, the divine aspect of your life on earth becomes manifest and obvious. This vision, however, is never possible without a kind of death, a farewell to everything you have loved, a giving away of all that is dear to you.

The invitation to this dance is more common than we realize, but it is not always obvious. The sacrifice it demands is not accompanied by disenchantment from the monastic world. It affects no airs of disdain or disassociation. Perhaps the only note is a sort of quiet joy. Yet the invitation is not always accepted. Monks hug the walls when they should be dancing. Or worse yet, they disappear down the road thinking the place is not for them

One sees this pattern in so many places and in so many life-situations that we ought not see it with surprise in the monastic life: life to death to greater life. One seems eternally called and beckoned to greater joy and then when the joy is attained one is beckoned further, but only at the price of present surrender. In the surrender the heart is almost broken.

One sees it in individuals, in families, in communities, in nations. The law of death is writ large in the law of life and Calvary is not exceptional but typical. It is a pattern of life: we live by dying.

It is hard to see how Tibet and the way of life Tibetans knew there can survive the present death. Still, you never know. There have been times in history when people were expecting holy Church to breathe her last breath and were certain they had heard the rattle of death in her throat.

We must call on God often for the courage to die, to give everything away, to hold nothing back. If we are alive it is most certain that we are to die. But death is not once; it is something that appears almost as a constant, as constant as the daily sleep in which we die a while every day. There is some strange death in the life of a monk by which he dies to his monastic life. It is different with each one and yet adapted to each one. In almost every case we expect it to fit as neatly as eggs fit into an egg box.

This means we must be wary of our loves and speak softly of things that mean much to us. What will be taken from us will be what we love most, not least. It is those who love the monastic life most who will be torn from it in some strange way.

One can only think of Dom Vital.

Dom Vital was a former abbot of a monastery in Belgium. He was elected abbot when young and served only a few years when for various reasons, including post-World War I politics, he was compelled to resign. Thus he was a retired abbot early in life in a time when retired abbots continued to wear cross and ring. Eventually he moved to the United States to live out his life at Gethsemani.

Humanly speaking, there could have been little in life that Dom Vital enjoyed as much as being an abbot. He was kind, genial, spiritual, loved every nook and cranny of monastic life, and was fond of rite, ritual, rubric, ceremony, incense, vesture, and monastic protocol. One thing after another that he loved was stripped from him.

In his last years the Gethsemani he loved was being torn down around him. His dearly loved Latin liturgy was slowly being displaced, and all the ancient melodies that so haunted his soul were never to be heard again. When they tore down the old steeple it is sure that his heart broke, for he died soon after. There is no doubt that he hoped at least that he would be given a fine funeral, a pontifical with all the trimmings befitting a retired abbot who was so every bit a monk. Alas, the abbot was not home, the church was in shambles from remodeling, and we had to use a temporary chapel on the third floor up under the roof. It was hardly handsome and no place for any ceremony of size or dignity.

There we sang Dom Vital's requiem, the prior officiating. It was the best we could do and was poor enough. Afterwards we went down three flights of stairs and took him out to the cemetery and buried him. It was the last humbling, it was stripping. It was hard to miss. One could but wince and shake one's head. The lesson was not lost on us. We know that Dom Vital dances now in the kingdom in full regalia with a splendor that puts to shame earthly pontificalia.

Die we must then. May we die well and, that we may do so, let us die a bit each day. To do that we have but to live. Take each day as it comes, see the Lord in all that happens and have a kind of response to the will of God that is much like dancing. You must work with it. It is not a matter of passive submission. This is no way to dance; it is too heavy, too leaden, too dragging and uninspired. No, you must dance with your partner, you must cooperate, you must work with the will of God. This is the sort of dancing that leads to the kingdom and makes one free. As you dance you are quite aware that everything you know, everything you love, everything you have is being taken away from you. You keep right on dancing, for it matters not. Meanwhile you see the heavens opening and behold the Son of Man in glory.

❧ SEASONAL HOMILIES

A Homily on Labor ❧

This homily was preached by Father Kelty at a mass on Labor Day 1967, in honor of Saint Joseph for the craftsmen who just completed the renovation of the monastic church of the Abbey of Gethsemani.

YESTERDAY, in a very splendid action, our reverend archbiship consecrated this holy stone which is the altar of the abbey church of Gethsemani. Beneath, first, were buried the bones of saints and martyrs to testify to the Christian's call to holiness and martyrdom. Then it was washed with blessed water, annointed with sacred chrism and finally, in a vision of glory, at each corner and in the middle was marked for the five wounds of Christ with flames of fire, with the fragrance of incense. Then the Mass of the Assumption of the Mother of God was offered on it by the community. And so this monastery makes a new beginning.

But beginnings are always rooted in the past. There is a cross on a hilltop not far from here that means much to us. It is the cross that once stood on the steeple high above this holy spot. When the renovation of this church began, it was not without some anxiety that the monks realized that the steeple had to come down, nor without anguish that they watched the workmen first begin the demolition. But it became evident very soon that there was no need for anxiety or anguish, for from the men themselves came a tender, spontaneous reverence for the cross that made everyone glad. They lowered it slowly, inch by inch, never allowing it to be any way but upright, in honor and dignity all the way down to the ground. Then, rather than destroy it, we decided to erect it on a hill in the woods around us. There today it looks out over Gethsemani as it has done for over one hundred years, placed in a lovely setting, marked with a plaque.

There is another cross from the past. It is this cross our founding fathers brought from the mother house in France when they left that monastery in 1848 to found a new abbey in the wilderness of Kentucky. This cross is our link to our mother, perhaps the only material thing we have, save the bones of the monks, that identifies us with our forebears. It is not inappropriate that we should do honor to such a cross, unworthy of such men though we be.

Nor should it escape anyone that both crosses are bare; they have no body. Maybe we ought to use bare crosses for a while. Maybe we need to be reminded that Jesus is perhaps tired of hanging there and wants us to take our turn. Maybe we need to see in imagery the truth that there is no Christianity without the cross, and that there is no Christian unless he knows what it is to carry it and, better than that, to be nailed to it. Monks need to be reminded of this, for they too are tempted to take to their heels when they hear the sound of the hammer and the clink of nails, the very things that will make their identity with Christ total.

We thank you for your work on this church and on the preau and the cloister. We thank in particular William Shickel and his associates, for from his creative mind came what you see today. Who would have thought the old bricks and beams had so much beauty in them?

We hope your work here these few months will be a joy to you all your lives, that you will tell your sons and grandsons after them, 'I worked on the church of the Abbey of Gethsemani'.

And we, our part?

May we never give you cause for shame or regret. May we be the men God called us to be, men of prayer and peace. And men of work. Monks have always been men of work, of labor. You have only to look at their hands to see that this is so. We know, then, and love the world of labor since work is a share in the creative genius of God and a carrying out of our part of his plan.

Just as the redemption is not finished and must be completed by people strong in love who are able and willing to take up a cross, carry it to the end, and then be nailed to it and die on it, so too the world is not finished. It must be completed by those who will take the world as they know it and somehow make it better, holier, happier, and more beautiful than when they found it, who measure happiness not by what they can get but by what they can give, who are not ashamed to be wounded in the service of love, knowing that such wounds will one day be blazing in glory in the fire of God's love.

Today we gather round this altar to offer the Eucharist in honor of the father of the Holy Family, Joseph the Carpenter. May he bless us all and may he especially bless you and your families for your work here for us. Never forget that you are and always will be a part of this place. You have left your mark behind you. Part of you is here. God grant it to be eternal joy.

Blessed be St Joseph, Father of
The Holy Family

Easter and Brother Jerome ᔆ

Yesterday I saw two daffodils happily blooming in a warm corner of the wall behind the novices' garden. This morning, I must report, they look a little discouraged. In fact, things look a little askew in many corners. Last night when we went to fetch the fire from the rock there was a hint of rain on my face, and the skies were very dark. We could see no moon. Perhaps it was just as well for it would have been a sad moon anyway, far from full paschal glory, since lunar and solar calendars this year are at odds.

If the fire was handsome, and it was, I was more fascinated by the generously proportioned sparks and embers that a stiff wind out of the north seemed to blow right through the monks and out over the crosses of our dead. Then we rose this Easter to find that the white shroud we laid over Brother Jerome now covers the earth. Or better, we found that the white cloths lying in the empty tomb are about us everywhere. I found the woods enchantingly lovely in white this wintry-spring Resurrection Day.

Things are, then, somewhat askew. One feels this is the way it was for Peter and John. They had been through this harrowing of Christ's disgraceful death and now this. They believed, John says in his gospel, but he softens it somewhat in a sort of plea for tenderness, 'For they did not as yet know the Scriptures.' Alas, even when they did it would be hard enough.

And this I take to be the lesson. Your life and mine, the life of the community, the life of the church, this country, the world, will more often than not be at odds, mixed up, askew. This is about the way it is, and faith is not to make it all good again. Faith is not to set it all right, tidy it up, organize and explain it.

112

No, faith impregnates this chaos with divine life which is a long time
in birthing. So we keep our cool. Brother Jerome got the message. Maybe it was because he knew the Scriptures. He knew serenity, he knew
peace, he knew joy, he knew love, and he lived among us and our madness. Now he sleeps beneath white cover. But, he will soon rise, as will
we all, because Christ has risen from the dead. In that even daffodils take
courage, and you, and I.

Three Wise Men 🐦

I F YOU WANT TO KNOW a people you must learn the songs they sing, the stories they tell, the dreams they dream. This is true of any people. So, on this Feast of the Three Wise Men I have taken from the world three men we sing about, tell stories about, and dream about, to see what they can manifest to us as monks.

The first of these three men is Abraham Lincoln, born in Kentucky. What is the meaning of this great man? What does his life say? Stand with me for a moment in his classic memorial in Washington and look up into the face of that figure with the reverent people who are always found there. What is his significance? Is it not perhaps integrity, sincerity? Does he not represent courage, strength, along with kindness and tenderness? Does he not illustrate the loneliness and anguish of responsibility, the life of dedication, but perhaps most of all, human compassion and mercy, a great love for his fellows? I think this is what he means.

Take another, figure whose memory is perhaps less well-defined, not so accurately drawn, but nonetheless, not without impact and influence. I refer to Daniel Boone. Boone signifies in a very real way the spirit of the pioneer, the one who leaves behind the comfort and ease of the good life and goes forth into the wilderness, into the unknown, to seek out new paths to the other side of the mountain. He symbolizes the desire to lead others to a new world, to make the way clear for them in a life characterized by difficulty and hardship in the midst of God's great virgin land.

The third man is not an individual; he is a composite, an amalgam drawn from countless historical examples. The influence of his ideal, his idea, perhaps exerts more force today among our own people and all over the world, than at any other time. I refer, of course, to the American cowboy. What is the meaning of this strange figure that has so powerful, so dramatic an appeal? He probably comes closest to anything like a valid symbol of what we might call the spirit of our people and our land.

It is important to see this. There is scarcely need to point out that the cowboy is our version of the shepherd. He herds cattle on horseback. No one would pretend that all cowboys are holy people, nor were all shepherds holy in our Lord's day. Yet Christ did not hesitate to call himself the Good Shepherd. It is not strange, then, that so many of the shepherd's good qualities live on in the cowboy.

What does the cowboy mean? He means the great open spaces, the great sky above, the stars at night. He means the wild prairie, rolling out on all sides, the great mountains in the distance. He means a love for his horse, for his herd, for all living things. He is lean and hard and ascetic, yet he is tender and soft-spoken. He will speak up and fight for what is right and good, even to the death. Yet in all this he is detached; there is no personal benefit in it for him. He solves problems and then rides off into the distance. His life is simple and uncluttered, just his boots and saddles. He is a lone figure, a celibate, he never marries.

These three figures are of significance. Add them up and what do you get? You have a person of integrity and conviction filled with compassion. You have a hardy, disciplined individual willing to leave behind a comfortable and reassuring kind of life for one that involves risk, danger, enterprise, in an endeavor to find a way to a new land, to open a road for others to follow. You have someone who is the partner of God's great natural world, the lone figure who loves all living things, who will fight for what is right, yet in a detached, unselfish way.

Who is this composite man? What is he if not a dream that every person harbors in the heart? Everyone has this great desire to be better, this haunting awareness that one is called to a greater reality, a dream of some new kind of person, a new Adam. It is a vision, indeed, of Christ.

That is why the people of our land love the monk once they come to know him. In some ways our life says what they themselves would like to say. It is appropriate that this first Trappist-Cistercian abbey in the new land should be established here in this corner of Kentucky, in the birthplace of Lincoln and the heart of Daniel Boone country, and that this monastery should first come to the attention of many people through a book about a cowboy who became a monk.* Surely there is meaning in this working of Providence.

It seems clear enough to me that the American soul has a contemplative quality. Our songs, our tales, our dreams show it. The three figures of Lincoln, Boone, and the cowboy all have a kind of simple relation to God, expressed at once in a certain spirit of solitude together with a great love of humanity, a solitude in which reality is found and love expressed. Perhaps this marks the beginning of a contemplative tradition in America. If so, we must continue to do our best to leave after us a valid tradition, that we live a life with which a contemplative soul can identify in his own heart, a life close to God and to man and to reality.

It is through faith that we live such a life, a life at once communal and solitary. Our faith tells us that every person is a brother or sister of Christ, a child of God. That, in a very real sense, every individual is Christ, has Christ hidden within. This is the faith we live by, the heart of our life.

✓ We know that faith is the most potent force in the world for by faith we realize that which we believe. When I see Christ in others something very remarkable happens. By my faith I bring about a great good. I touch the greatest reality within them and they respond with their whole being. I touch something and they come to life. I have told them in so many words what they knew all along and had not the courage to believe, that Christ lives in them. By my faith in Christ I make Christ manifest. ~~ also ~~~ regard to angels

So many people seem to go through the world groping, struggling, stumbling in darkness. They have a light within, but they do not understand it, they do not trust it. They misinterpret, doubt, and hesitate. But here and there, now and then, they see something that sets the flame burning brightly: an idea, an image, a song, a tale, a dream. They take hold of it. They see the nobility of Lincoln's great compassion, Boone's courageous spirit, the cowboy's simple awareness and goodness and beauty. They come to know what faith is, to see with the heart into the

*Father Raymond, OSCO, *The Man Who Got Even With God* (Milwaukee, 1941).

reality of all things. The very sight of it awakens their own hearts, and they come to believe again in the goodness hidden within them.

The first Wise Men manifested Christ by looking for him. We also seek Christ. We seek him in one another, in the poor, the workers, our guests. We seek him in Kentucky, in history. We seek him in Lincoln and in Boone and in the cowboy. There is no sacred and secular to God. All is sacred in him.

That is why I chose three figures from the world of everyday rather than from the world of Scripture or Breviary or Missal. It is not hard to see God in a person who has been canonized or in consecrated bread. A monk, however, sees God in all that is. If you cannot see Christ in Lincoln, can you see him in me? If not in Boone, can you see him in the person who hauls your coal? If you cannot see him in Kentucky, can you see him at all, in any place, in any history? He is in all that is real.

It is faith, this seeing God, that makes him manifest. It is this way that we are in turn wise people of our own day and in our land make possible an epiphany of God simply by being what we are. There is surely no greater joy than to know that you manifest God by seeing him in faith in all things everywhere.

The great fruit of the liturgical revival which has followed the Second Vatican Council will, I hope, not be just a development of togetherness in worship or a new sense of personal involvement in works of charity and zeal. Our people will take these things in stride without much ado. Rather, I pray that the fruit of liturgical renewal will be the encounter of the individual soul with God in a vital way never before experienced, penetrating to the very roots of humanity. In such an encounter saints are born. In a liturgy that is doing what it ought, the soul will stand before its Maker and that soul will either run away or become the soul of a saint.

It is much like our own life. It is not just being here together in a monastery that effects much. It is in the encounter with God that saints are born. The framework of our life makes this possible: our prayer, our work, our reading, our silence, our life in common—everything is set up for the encounter. You can have it if you want it. In the end, of course, it is the monk himself and he only who decides whether or not he will embrace reality.

Christ, then, is the song we sing, the tale we tell, the dream we dream. He is the great reality in us and around us, the Christ who daily grows more manifest until that last great day when, in one dazzling moment, the final epiphany, it will be made clear to all that Christ is the heart of everything.

CISTERCIAN TEXTS

Bernard of Clairvaux

- Apologia to Abbot William
- Five Books on Consideration: Advice to a Pope
- Homilies in Praise of the Blessed Virgin Mary
- In Praise of the New Knighthood
- Letters of Bernard of Clairvaux / by B.S. James
- Life and Death of Saint Malachy the Irishman
- Love without Measure: Extracts from the Writings of St Bernard / by Paul Dimier
- On Grace and Free Choice
- On Loving God / Analysis by Emero Stiegman
- Parables and Sentences
- Sermons for the Summer Season
- Sermons on Conversion
- Sermons on the Song of Songs I–IV
- The Steps of Humility and Pride

William of Saint Thierry

- The Enigma of Faith
- Exposition on the Epistle to the Romans
- Exposition on the Song of Songs
- The Golden Epistle
- The Mirror of Faith
- The Nature and Dignity of Love
- On Contemplating God: Prayer & Meditations

Aelred of Rievaulx

- Dialogue on the Soul
- Liturgical Sermons, I
- The Mirror of Charity
- Spiritual Friendship
- Treatises I: On Jesus at the Age of Twelve, Rule for a Recluse, The Pastoral Prayer
- Walter Daniel: The Life of Aelred of Rievaulx

Gertrud the Great of Helfta

- Spiritual Exercises
- The Herald of God's Loving-Kindness (Books 1, 2)
- The Herald of God's Loving-Kindness (Book 3)

John of Ford

- Sermons on the Final Verses of the Songs of Songs I–VII

Gilbert of Hoyland

- Sermons on the Songs of Songs I–III
- Treatises, Sermons and Epistles

Other Early Cistercian Writers

- Adam of Perseigne, Letters of
- Alan of Lille: The Art of Preaching
- Amadeus of Lausanne: Homilies in Praise of Blessed Mary
- Baldwin of Ford: The Commendation of Faith
- Baldwin of Ford: Spiritual Tractates I–II
- Geoffrey of Auxerre: On the Apocalypse
- Guerric of Igny: Liturgical Sermons Vol. 1 & 2
- Helinand of Froidmont: Verses on Death
- Idung of Prüfening: Cistercians and Cluniacs: The Case for Cîteaux
- In the School of Love. An Anthology of Early Cistercian Texts
- Isaac of Stella: Sermons on the Christian Year, I–[II]
- The Life of Beatrice of Nazareth
- Serlo of Wilton & Serlo of Savigny: Seven Unpublished Works
- Stephen of Lexington: Letters from Ireland
- Stephen of Sawley: Treatises
- Three Treatises on Man: A Cistercian Anthropology

MONASTIC TEXTS

Eastern Monastic Tradition

- Abba Isaiah of Scete: Ascetic Discourses
- Besa: The Life of Shenoute
- Cyril of Scythopolis: Lives of the Monks of Palestine
- Dorotheos of Gaza: Discourses and Sayings
- Evagrius Ponticus: Praktikos and Chapters on Prayer
- Handmaids of the Lord: Lives of Holy Women in Late Antiquity & the Early Middle Ages
- Harlots of the Desert
- John Moschos: The Spiritual Meadow
- Lives of the Desert Fathers
- Lives of Simeon Stylites
- Manjava Skete
- Mena of Nikiou: Isaac of Alexandra & St Macrobius
- The Monastic Rule of Iosif Volotsky (Revised Edition)
- Pachomian Koinonia I–III
- Paphnutius: Histories/Monks of Upper Egypt
- The Sayings of the Desert Fathers
- The Spiritually Beneficial Tales of Paul, Bishop of Monembasia
- Symeon the New Theologian: The Theological and Practical Treatises & The Three Theological Discourses
- Theodoret of Cyrrhus: A History of the

Monks of Syria
* The Syriac Fathers on Prayer and the Spiritual Life

Western Monastic Tradition

* Achard of Saint Victor: Works
* Anselm of Canterbury: Letters I–III / by Walter Fröhlich
* Bede: Commentary…Acts of the Apostles
* Bede: Commentary…Seven Catholic Epistles
* Bede: Homilies on the Gospels I–II
* Bede: Excerpts from the Works of Saint Augustine on the Letters of the Blessed Apostle Paul
* The Celtic Monk
* Gregory the Great: Forty Gospel Homilies
* Life of the Jura Fathers
* The Maxims of Stephen of Muret
* Peter of Celle: Selected Works
* The Letters of Armand Jean-deRancé I–II
* Rule of the Master
* Rule of Saint Augustine

CHRISTIAN SPIRITUALITY

* A Cloud of Witnesses…The Development of Christian Doctrine / by David N. Bell
* The Call of Wild Geese / by Matthew Kelty
* The Cistercian Way / by André Louf
* The Contemplative Path
* Drinking From the Hidden Fountain / by Thomas Spidlík
* Entirely for God / by Elizabeth Isichei
* Eros and Allegory: Medieval Exegesis of the Song of Songs / by Denys Turner
* Fathers Talking / by Aelred Squire
* Friendship and Community / by Brian McGuire
* Grace Can do Moore: Spiritual Accompaniment / by André Louf
* High King of Heaven / by Benedicta Word
* How Far to Follow / by B. Olivera
* The Hermitage Within / by a Monk
* Life of St Mary Magdalene and of Her Sister St Martha / by David Mycoff
* The Luminous Eye / by Sebastian Brock
* Many Mansions / by David N. Bell
* Mercy in Weakness / by André Louf
* The Name of Jesus / by Irénée Hausherr
* No Moment Too Small / by Norvene Vest
* Penthos: The Doctrine of Compunction in the Christian East / by Irénée Hausherr
* Praying the Word / by Enzo Bianchi
* Praying with Benedict / by Korneel Vermeiren
* Russian Mystics / by Sergius Bolshakoff
* Sermons in a Monastery / by Matthew Kelty

* Silent Herald of Unity: The Life of Maria Gabrielle Sagheddu / by Martha Driscoll
* Spiritual Direction in the Early Christian East / by Irénée Hausherr
* The Spirituality of the Christian East / by Thomas Spidlík
* The Spirituality of the Medieval West / by André Vauchez
* The Spiritual World of Isaac the Syrian / by Hilarion Alfeyev
* Tuning In To Grace / by André Louf

MONASTIC STUDIES

* Community and Abbot in the Rule of St Benedict I–II / by Adalbert de Vogüé
* The Hermit Monks of Grandmont / by Carole A. Hutchison
* In the Unity of the Holy Spirit / by Sighard Kleiner
* A Life Pleasing to God: Saint Basil's Monastic Rules / By Augustine Holmes
* Memoirs [of Jean Leclercq]: From Grace to Grace
* Monastic Practices / by Charles Cummings
* The Occupation of Celtic Sites in Ireland / by Geraldine Carville
* Reading St Benedict / by Adalbert de Vogüé
* Rule of St Benedict: A Doctrinal and Spiritual Commentary / by Adalbert de Vogüé
* The Venerable Bede / by Benedicta Ward
* Western Monasticism / by Peter King
* What Nuns Read / by David N. Bell

CISTERCIAN STUDIES

* Aelred of Rievaulx: A Study / by Aelred Squire
* Athirst for God: Spiritual Desire in Bernard of Clairvaux's Sermons on the Song of Songs / by Michael Casey
* Beatrice of Nazareth in Her Context / by Roger De Ganck
* Bernard of Clairvaux: Man, Monk, Mystic / by Michael Casey [tapes and readings]
* Catalogue of Manuscripts in the Obrecht Collection of the Institute of Cistercian Studies / by Anna Kirkwood
* Christ the Way: The Christology of Guerric of Igny / by John Morson
* The Cistercians in Denmark / by Brian McGuire
* The Cistercians in Scandinavia / by James France
* A Difficult Saint / by Brian McGuire
* The Finances of the Cistercian Order in the Fourteenth Century / by Peter King

- Fountains Abbey and Its Benefactors
  / by Joan Wardrop
- A Gathering of Friends: Learning & Spirituality
  in John of Ford / by Costello and Holdsworth
- The Golden Chain...Isaac of Stella /
  byBernard Mc Ginn
- Image and Likeness: Augustinian Spirituality
  of William of St Thierry / by David Bell
- Index of Authors & Works in Cistercian
  Libraries in Great Britain I / by David Bell
- Index of Cistercian Authors and Works in
  Medieval Library Catalogues in Great Britian
  / by David Bell
- The Mystical Theology of St Bernard
  / by Étienne Gilson
- The New Monastery: Texts & Studies on the
  Earliest Cistercians
- Monastic Odyssey / by Marie Kervingant
- Nicolas Cotheret's Annals of Cîteaux
  / by Louis J. Lekai
- Pater Bernhardus: Martin Luther and
  Bernard of Clairvaux / by Franz Posset
- Pathway of Peace / by Charles Dumont
- Rancé and the Trappist Legacy
  / by A. J. Krailsheimer
- A Second Look at Saint Bernard
  / by Jean Leclercq
- The Spiritual Teachings of St Bernard of
  Clairvaux / by John R. Sommerfeldt
- Studies in Medieval Cistercian History
- Three Founders of Cîteaux
  / by Jean-Baptiste Van Damme
- Towards Unification with God (Beatrice of
  Nazareth in Her Context, 2)
- William, Abbot of St Thierry
- Women and St Bernard of Clairvaux
  / by Jean Leclercq

MEDIEVAL RELIGIOUS WOMEN

A Sub-series edited by
Lillian Thomas Shank and John A. Nichols
- Distant Echoes
- Hidden Springs: Cistercian Monastic Women
  (2 volumes)
- Peace Weavers

CARTHUSIAN TRADITION

- The Call of Silent Love / by A Carthusian
- The Freedom of Obedience / by A Carthusian
- From Advent to Pentecost / by A Carthusian
- Guigo II: The Ladder of Monks & Twelve
  Meditations / by E. Colledge & J. Walsh
- Halfway to Heaven / by R.B. Lockhart
- Interior Prayer / by A Carthusian

- Meditations of Guigo I / by A. Gordon Mursall
- The Prayer of Love and Silence / by A Carthusian
- Poor, Therefore Rich / by A Carthusian
- They Speak by Silences / by A Carthusian
- The Way of Silent Love (A Carthusian Miscellany)
- Where Silence is Praise / by A Carthusian
- The Wound of Love (A Carthusian Miscellany)

CISTERCIAN ART, ARCHITECTURE & MUSIC

- Cistercian Abbeys of Britain
- Cistercian Europe / by Terryl N. Kinder
- Cistercians in Medieval Art / by James France
- Studies in Medieval Art and Architecture
  / edited by Meredith Parsons Lillich
  (Volumes II–V are now available)
- Stones Laid Before the Lord
  / by Anselme Dimier
- Treasures Old and New: Nine Centuries of
  Cistercian Music (compact disc and cassette)

THOMAS MERTON

- The Climate of Monastic Prayer / by T. Merton
- Legacy of Thomas Merton / by P. Hart
- Message of Thomas Merton / by P. Hart
- Monastic Journey of Thomas Merton
  / by Patrick Hart
- Thomas Merton/Monk / by P. Hart
- Thomas Merton on St Bernard
- Toward an Integrated Humanity
  / edited by M. Basil Pennington

CISTERCIAN LITURGICAL DOCUMENTS SERIES

- Cistercian Liturgical Documents Series
  / edited by Chrysogonus Waddell, ocso
- Hymn Collection from the...Paraclete
- The Paraclete Statutes:: Institutiones nostrae
- Molesme Summer-Season Breviary (4 vol.)
- Old French Ordinary & Breviary of the
  Abbey of the Paraclete (2 volumes)
- Twelfth-century Cistercian Hymnal (2 vol.)
- The Twelfth-century Cistercian Psalter
- Two Early Cistercian Libelli Missarum

FESTSCHRIFTS

- Bernardus Magister...Nonacentenary of the Birth of St Bernard
- The Joy of Learning & the Love of God: Essays in Honor of Jean Leclercq
- Praise no Less Than Charity in honor of C. Waddell
- Studiosorum Speculumin honor of Louis J. Lekai
- Truth As Gift... in honor of J. Sommerfeldt

BUSINESS INFORMATION

Editorial Offices & Customer Service

- Cistercian Publications
  WMU Station, 1903 West Michigan Avenue
  Kalamazoo, Michigan 49008-5415   USA

  Telephone 616 387 8920
  Fax   616 387 8390
  e-mail   cistpub@wmich.edu

Please Note: As of 13 July 2002 the 616 area code becomes 269

Canada

- Novalis
  49 Front Street East, Second Floor
  Toronto, Ontario M5E 1B3   CANADA

  Telephone 1 800 204 4140
  Fax   416 363 9409

U.K.

- Cistercian Publications UK
  Mount Saint Bernard Abbey
  Coalville, Leicestershire LE67 5UL   UK

- UK Customer Service & Book Orders
  Cistercian Publications
  97 Loughborough Road
  Thringstone, Coalville
  Leicestershire LE67 8LQ   UK

  Telephone 01530 45 27 24
  Fax   01530 45 02 10
  e-mail   MsbcistP@aol.com

Website

- www.spencerabbey.org/cistpub

Trade Accounts & Credit Applications

- Cistercian Publications / Accounting
  6219 West Kistler Road
  Ludington, Michigan 49431   USA

  Fax   231 843 8919

Cistercian Publications is a non-profit corporation. Its publishing program is restricted to monastic texts in translation and books on the monastic tradition.

A complete catalogue of texts in translation and studies on early, medieval, and modern monasticism is available, free of charge, from any of the addresses above.